A Redcatcher's
Letters from Nam

A **Redcatcher's**
Letters from Nam

Book 2

REFLECTIONS OF FAMILY AND FRIENDS

Written by

Patricia Farawell Enyedy

authorHOUSE®

AuthorHouse™
1663 Liberty Drive
Bloomington, IN 47403
www.authorhouse.com
Phone: 1 (800) 839-8640

Published by AuthorHouse 04/06/2016

ISBN: 978-1-5049-5447-1 (sc)
ISBN: 978-1-5049-5446-4 (e)

Print information available on the last page.

Any people depicted in stock imagery provided by Thinkstock are models, and such images are being used for illustrative purposes only. Certain stock imagery © Thinkstock.

This book is printed on acid-free paper.

TABLE OF CONTENTS

PART 2

This book is dedicated to the 199th
Light Infantry Brigade
In loving memory of my brother
PFC George Thomas Farawell
And all the brave men and women
Who lost their lives or were wounded in Vietnam.
Thank you to the living vets who
never forgot their buddies.
May it bring you some peace to know
The families of the KIA's or MIA's
never forgot you either.
You could have been our boy.
I thank you one and all.
God Bless You.
Check out their website: www.redcatcher.org

ACKNOWLEDGEMENTS

Thank you for your help from the 199th LIB: Clay Crowder, for your wonderful memorial in memory of George and giving me direction; Bob Fromme, for your patience and guidance by letting me read your letters; Tom Hays for permission to use the patch, memorial and information of the 199th and Ricky Jones and Larry Spaulding for your kind emails.

Thank you for your reflections:

Wayne Garrett 199th LIB D 4/12, Stephen Farawell, Richard (Gag) and Jennifer Gagliardi, Ronnie Kisylia, Richard Burke, Barbara Lyons Pawlowski, Steven Di Gangi, Edward Malinowsky, Diane Stracensky Pribush, Robin Kornmeyer, Paul Schlicker, Sam Iacobone, Doug Jolly, Michael Favor and Mike Brown.

Special thanks to:

My nephew Major L. A. (Jack) McLaughlin Jr., US Army for saying those words, "Aunt Patti you should publish these letters" and helping me edit. Elliott Enyedy, my husband, who thinks I can do anything I put my mind to. My brother Stephen for his support who helped me find the "guys" who along with me loved finding out more information about our brother. To my family for all their prayers and support who can tell you what they were doing when they heard the news. To my friends, who have listened to this story so many times and we still cry every time. To Richie Gag, my dear friend, who loved my brother as much as I did. Tom and Cheryl Snyder of C&T Artworks for designing this beautiful cover.

Thank you all for helping me find the closure, I needed at this time.

PREFACE

My brother PFC George T. Farawell was sent to Vietnam in January 1969. After the holidays with 8 weeks of basic training at Fort Dix, NJ and 8 weeks in Fort Polk, LA of Advanced Infantry Training our 19-year-old boy was off to Vietnam half way around the world. They had a 3-day stop over in San Francisco where the future veterans had a great time, their last fling before going to war.

Our boy was off on his own for the first time in his life. I call George "boy" in my book because that is what he was. Time has stood still in my memory of him. I know when he stepped off that plane in Vietnam, he was a man but in our hearts he is still our boy.

The Army gave him an M16 and he was assigned to the 199th Light Infantry Brigade, Delta Company 4/12. There he would live the last 8 weeks of his life, afraid, dirty, bug bitten, in a foreign land with strangers who were now his lifeline.

My brother wrote 25 wonderful letters to mom, dad, my husband and myself in those 8 short weeks. In this book, I will share his letters. These precious letters faded with time, some written in pencil and on all different types of paper always trying to reassure us he was ok. If your loved one did not write, these could be your letters.

This book has taken quite a few turns since I started writing it. My first intention was to find Glenn, George's bunker buddy who was wounded on 16 March 69. I still have not found him.

George and I were only 15 months apart and we were so close, we even shared a best friend. Richard and I kept in touch over the years. I was reading George's letters recently and thought no one else has ever read these. I wanted to share them with family and his friends. What happened to all of his friends?

I decided I would try and find everyone. It was not that difficult since most of them are still in NJ. I found them one at a time. Once the shock wore off and the tears stopped flowing they were so pleased with what I intended to do. One led me to another. They were all eager to talk about emotions that have been buried for 32 years. I wanted to know how they all found out, what happened in their life. So we met one Saturday afternoon at George's Park to reflect and have dinner. This was hard on me because I still think of them as 19 like my brother. I met all these wonderful men and women who never forgot their friend. They all have **"visited George"** at the "Park", the DC Memorial, or the NJ memorial in the last 6 months.

They have all written a **"reflection of their friend"** 32 years later. They are priceless just like their friend's letters.

BOOK I
THE SOLDIER

For us lay people I wanted to give you a
little background on the 199th.

THE BEGINNING OF THE 199TH LIB

Formally activated June 1st, 1966 the Brigade began small unit training on June 27th at Fort Benning, Georgia to be followed by eight weeks of field training at Camp Shelby, Mississippi. Fulfilling the concept of a modern Light Infantry Brigade **("Light Swift & Accurate" is the 199th's motto)** and its role in counterinsurgency warfare the Brigade was designed as **a hitchhiker unit with heavy equipment kept to a minimum.**

Following intensive preparations, a 280-man advance party left in early November 1966. After final review the majority of Redcatchers were flown to Oakland, California where they boarded the USS Sultan and the USS Pope for the more than two weeks trip across the Pacific Ocean. The USS Sultan docked at Vung Tau and two days later the USS Pope docked and everyone moved to meet the advanced party at a tent encampment north of Long Binh that was to become the Brigade Main Base, Camp Frenzell-Jones.

REDCATCHER 199TH MEMORIAL
(199th Infantry Brigade) Memorial
Dedication May 24, 1998
The Memorial is located at Fort Benning, Columbus Ga.
Just in front of the Infantry Museum.

REDCATCHER THE 199TH PATCH

Chances are most people cannot tell you what
the Redcatcher patch stands for.
The Blue and White denote the Infantry.
The Spear, an early Infantry weapon, in flames symbolizes
the evolution and firepower of the modern Infantry.
It represents early Infantry's use of thrusting weapons and
projectiles thrown or shot from bows, ballista's and catapults.
Contrary to popular belief, the RED BALL in the center of the patch
represents man's splitting of the atom, the Nuclear Age in which
Infantry fights side by side with weapons of sophisticated warfare.
The Yellow flame signifies the advent of gunpowder
and the new trend in Infantry warfare.
Fusillades through the centuries echoed from reports of the
matchlock, the flintlock, the percussion cap and repeating rifle.
Infantry warfare becomes more massive in the
face of these weapons, but the repeating rifle
dominates, with modifications, to this day.
The overall patch is symbolic of the development of
Infantry and Infantry support through the ages.
The oblong blue shield of the patch is a depiction of
the shields used by the forerunners of modern Infantry,
namely the Greek Phalanx and Roman Legion.

GEORGE THOMAS FARAWELL

**Company D.
4th Battalion 12th Infantry Regiment
199th Light Infantry Brigade
PFC - E3 - Army - Selective Service
20 year old Single, Caucasian, Male
Born on Jan 27, 1949
From LINDEN, NEW JERSEY
His tour of duty began on Jan 19, 1969
Casualty was on Mar 18, 1969
in GIA DINH, SOUTH VIETNAM
Hostile, died of wounds
GROUND CASUALTY
OTHER EXPLOSIVE DEVICE
Body was recovered
Religion ROMAN CATHOLIC
Panel 29W - Line 68**

INTRODUCTION

PFC George T. Farawell
US 519 87070
199th Light Infantry Brigade
D 4/12

George was sent to Vietnam in January 1969. After a few days training in Long Binh he went into Delta Company the 199th LIB. He was stationed in Long Binh and died in Gia Dinh on the riverbank. He served as a radio telephone operator.

They had 6 men injured in his unit in 3 days, that week in March 1969 by stepping on land mines and tripping booby traps. George's bunker buddy, **Glenn** was the point man and since they were walking on the road turned off the metal detector. He only made one mistake. He tripped a booby trap. George saw it all. Glenn, suffered severe leg and feet injuries in the incident. George helped his injured buddy putting him in the helicopter. All those good men not hurt by enemy fire. I am not sure if any survived or if they knew George did not. I have been trying to find Glenn for years.

George wrote home that night to his family because he was so upset over the tragedies. He was trying to deal with his emotions. The following day, George was also injured on a land mine. He suffered a penetrating missile wound, right side of his chest, multi fragment wounds to chest, abdomen and left shoulder. He died on 18 March 1969. He was only in Vietnam for 8 weeks, 17 Jan 69 to 18 Mar 69. He just turned 20 years old on 27 Jan. He was buried with a Military funeral in Colonia, NJ. In our city of Linden NJ, George's death brought the death toll to 12.

George was awarded: **The Purple Heart, Army Commendation Medal, Good Conduct Medal, National Defense Service Medal, Vietnam Service Medal, Combat Infantryman Badge**, and the **Republic of Vietnam Campaign Ribbon** (awarded by the Republic of Vietnam).

The city of Linden, New Jersey dedicated a playground in his honor in September 1969 named PFC George T. Farawell Memorial Park. My parents were presented his medals at the ceremony.

George's name is inscribed on **the Vietnam Memorial in Washington DC**, and on the **Vietnam Memorial in Holmdel New Jersey** which was dedicated by General Norman Schwarzkopf. Gold families of the veterans were invited. We walked in a procession to the memorial lined with honor guards from around the state all branches of the military. Standing at attention sobbing servicemen saying "thank you" as we passed, some in wheelchairs, all proud and true Americans. It was a very emotional day.

George's name is also inscribed on the **199ᵗʰ Infantry Brigade Memorial** in Fort Benning Georgia I found out recently. He was a "redcatcher" never forgotten by the 199ᵗʰ LIB.

When you visit the memorials stop and "visit George" he is someone you would have been proud to know.

MY REFLECTIONS OF THE 199TH LIB

This is not a military book, it was never meant to be a military book. It is just a memoir of a soldier. These are only my impressions.

I have learned a lot in my research about the 199th Infantry. They are **"brothers"** who went through the worst time of their lives together. Can you imagine the constant fear of death for a year or two? Most of them fresh out of high school, from all different walks of life from farm boys to troubled teens who were put in the military over jail time. The officers were college graduates also taken from their homes and dropped in the middle of Vietnam to lead a group of young scared and some angry boys in war. They had to set an example for their unit and hope to God they made it.

The 199th did all foot patrol so they were in danger with every step they took. My brother wore out a pair of boots in 4 weeks. Land mines and booby traps were everywhere. You learned not to walk on the roads but through jungle, water and rice paddies with water up to your chin at times with everything they had held over their head. The 199th were the saviors who could not be saved. Their motto was Light Swift and Accurate.

They were taught to make buddies but not close friends in the war zone. The turnover time was too frequent. You could not mourn. There was no time you had to be ready for any possibility from enemy fire to tripping a booby trap. They went on ambush at night and walked in total darkness. You were responsible for the guy behind you to follow you or you could be lost for hours. You prayed the soldier on guard duty would stay awake during his watch. Your life was in his hands. They had to battle the extreme heat and they got use to being dirty real quick sometimes without a bath for weeks and some days without drinking water. One story I read during a rainstorm one soldier just striped down just to get clean with his soap. The rain let up before he could rinse but he felt clean. They learned to make do with whatever they had.

They had to battle insects, snakes, flies, fleas, ticks, termites, large beetles, roaches, leeches, red ants and even water buffalo just to name of few. They always had to check their boots before putting them on it was impossible to dry them out. They would put rubber bands on their pants to keep the leeches from crawling up their legs. If they did they would burn them off. In the river the red ants laid on the surface like red lace.

They had to do battle with people who all looked alike. Friends by day, enemy by night, they could trust no one except each other.

They had to battle bad press while still at war. Did my brother die in vain I think not, if one thing immerged from that fiasco was that it will never happen again! The American people want to know: who, what, where, when and why before our troops are sent to any conflict in the world.

Quite frankly, no one ever told me I could question or find out what happened. I never want to know what exactly happened I can guess from all the letters and information made available for me to read from some wonderful veterans who were there. It is bad enough the veterans have to carry that with them for the rest of their life but I do want them to know they served with a very special person in my life. They shared the last days of his precious life not me.

My mother for weeks had the number 18 in her head. That is day he died. Our precious boy was coming home a man. Never to be seen again by all who loved him but only in our memory. Now we had to deal with the numbness of his presence not being with us. We had to deal with the grief. Grief is not our friend, it takes you over, it makes you angry, and it goes away and comes back again. It never leaves you.

When a solider dies in combat, the pain is *deeper than death* on the families.

Right now writing this I feel so utterly helpless and spent with emotion 32 years later. Tears are flowing, hands are shaking and I want to scream. **Why? Why? Why?** Is the question we still ask today! Why my boy? What did he do to deserve this? Did he know what happened? Did he suffer? Did he get the best medical treatment? When my brother went to Vietnam I felt so guilty sleeping in a bed knowing George was in the jungle on the ground. It was worse then I imagined those bunkers along the river, dirty small bunkers, dirty water to bathe in, hot weather like an oven. You adjusted to it this was your life for the next year.

In finding the website www.redcatcher.org. I found answers to some of my haunting questions. Did he die alone? Did you look out for him the best you could? Did a fellow soldier see him get injured? Did he take a few minutes to reassure him that he would be fine, help to put him in the chopper and hope he lived? Did someone lovingly close his eyes for the last time? He was not just a body to transport, tag and send back to the States. He was a special person to many people and his death was going to change our lives forever. And it did.

After reading about the 199th Light Infantry Brigade I know they never would leave him alone or forget him after the war. He is still remembered today as a fellow redcatcher. George would be proud.

One day I was online and left my email in several locations trying to find Glenn.

I heard from Clay Crowder who introduced me to redcatcher website of the 199th. I left messages in trying to find anyone who may have known George or Glenn. I received the following messages from veterans, one who knew George, one who replaced him in the field and some just saying hello. Amazing all this info at your fingertips.

It was so emotional finding his fellow veterans of the 199th. I thank them all for their concern, help and sacrifice they made for our United States of America.

THANK YOU

With all the attention on WWII and Pearl Harbor right now, do something for me. It is never too late for recognition. If you know a soldier that served, pick up the phone, write a letter, and go visit him or her. These veterans have been living in hell since they went to Vietnam and most are still struggling in their own hell. They never forgot their buddies and we must never forget them.

I plan on being at the next Association meeting of the 199th in Arlington VA next Memorial Day. I want to meet these brave wonderful soldiers to shake their hand and say THANK YOU in person.

I know with each email they have to deal with emotions bringing brought to the surface to give the searching families information. We were just told he died and were given medals in his honor. The Army sent us a box with his boots in it. Imagine my parents opening that box where were all the things he requested to be sent, his camera, all the pictures he took, nothing came back to them.

In writing this book I hope to bring awareness of the heartbreak of saying good by, losing a loved one so young and dealing with the feeling of total helplessness and emotional devastation. The heartbreak of 32 years ago still aches, it never healed, and it only aches less.

May this book be a legacy for my children, family and friends. I know George lives on in their hearts as he does in mine. I want them to have the beautiful letters he wrote home. Being brave, scared, homesick, angry all at one time and writing letters trying to reassure us was not an easy task.

The other thing is how little our kids know about the Vietnam War. It is not covered in history, why is that? It did happen and affected almost every American's life we all new someone who went to Vietnam. It outrages me that it is the forgotten war.

One more thing, please never say to a veterans family, I would never let my son go into the military or not my boy! We heard this recently. We are a gold member family having lost someone in combat. Do you think we wanted him to go? Do you think we wanted him to face death every day for a year? That we loved our boy less because he went? Think about what the hell you just said and never say it again.

GETTING STARTED

This book has been in my thoughts for years. Five years ago, I started our Family Tree on my mother's side, which is no simple task with 530 people. I have been collecting essays from the family. The family reunion this year is focusing on first cousins, which are my brothers and me. It brought back so many cherished memories of my childhood and the missing brother who is in all our stories. I decided to explore my emotions, memories, and journey with my spirit to be touched again by my loving brother.

My nephew Major L.A. (Jack) Mc Laughlin US Army was visiting last Easter. He told me I could obtain George's military and medical records and find Glenn. I gave him the envelope to show him George's address. He asked to read the letter inside. He said "Aunt Patti you should publish these letters". He also said the 199th LIB was a very decorated elite unit. I told him it was something I always wanted to do and the seed was planted.

I am in the process of trying to find Glenn, George's buddy in Vietnam. It would be a wonderful postscript telling you I found him after all these years. I don't know if he survived or if he knew George did not make it.

We were lucky George was treated as a "Hero" when he came home. There was no negative press in our town. He was treated with dignity and respect. We are grateful.

I cannot say it any better than the following poem that was sent to me.

THE THINGS THEY CARRIED

They carried P-38 can openers and heat
tabs, watches and dog tags,
insect repellent, gum, cigarettes, Zippo lighters,
salt tablets, compress bandages,
ponchos, Kool-Aid, two to three canteens
of water, iodine tablets, sterno,
LRRP-rations, C-rations stuffed in socks.
They carried standard fatigues, jungle boots, bush hats,
flak jackets, and steel pots.
They carried the M-16 assault rifle.
They carried trip flares and Claymore mines, M-60 machine
guns, the M-79 grenade launcher, M-14s,
CAR-15s, Stoners, Swedish K's,
6mm Laws, shotguns, .45 caliber pistols,
silencers, the sound of bullets,
rockets, choppers, and sometimes the sound of silence.
They carried C-4 plastic explosives, an
assortment of hand grenades,
PRC-25 radios, knives and machetes.
Some carried napalm, CBU's, and large bombs;
some risked their lives to rescue others.
Some escaped the fear, but dealt with the death and damage.
Some made very hard decisions, and some just tried to survive.
They carried malaria, dysentery, ringworms, and leeches.
They carried the land itself as it hardened on their boots.
They carried stationery, pencils, and pictures of their
loved ones - real and imagined.
They carried love for people in the real
world, and love for one another.
And sometimes they disguised that love: "Don't mean nothin'!"

They carried memories.

For the most part, they carried themselves
with poise and a kind of dignity.
Now and then, there were times when panic set in, and
people squealed, or wanted to, but couldn't; When they
twitched and made moaning sounds and covered their
heads and said "Dear God", and hugged the earth and
fired their weapons blindly, and cringed and begged for the
noise to stop, and went wild and made stupid promises to
themselves and God and their parents, hoping not to die.
They carried the traditions of the United States military, and
memories and images of those who served before them.
They carried grief, terror, longing, and their reputations.
They carried the soldier's greatest fear:
the embarrassment of dishonor.
They crawled into tunnels, walked point, and advanced
under fire, so as not to die of embarrassment.
They were afraid of dying, but too afraid to show it.
They carried the emotional baggage of men and
women who might die at any moment.
They carried the weight of the world, and the
weight of every free citizen of America.

THEY CARRIED EACH OTHER! Amen
(Author Unknown)

REFLECTIONS OF FELLOW SOLDIERS IN 2001

June 29, 2001

Hi Patti:

My name is Clay Crowder and I served with the 199th Light Infantry Brigade in Vietnam. I did not know your brother but I wish I had known him. I am looking for a picture of your brother for my Honor Page on my site. My site is located at: http://recatcher10alpha.com/index2.htm. I honor a different soldier that was killed in action or still Missing in Action each month on my site. I sure would like to have a picture of your brother on the site. Take a look and see if you do not like the site it is ok but I think that it is the best site about the 199th Inf on the Internet so I have been told. It also has a Mini-Wall with all 755 that were killed in action while assigned to the 199th.

God Bless,
Clay Crowder
George's Honor Page is:
http://www.angelcities.com/members/redcatcher/farawell/farawell.htm

June 29, 2001

Patricia:

I remember **George Farawell he was with my unit in D4/12**. I was with D4/12 199th infantry from October 1968-October 1969. I remember when he joined our unit. I have thought about him many times over the years but was not aware that he died.

Vietnam was a hellhole a lot of booby traps that were very hard to detect until they were stepped on then it was to late. He was a brave young man as we were all young men at the time. He did is duty and was a good soldier. We went out on ambush patrol several times before he stepped on the land mine. A lot of times they would send us out at night walking long distances to reach our location to set up an Ambush. I know we all would cringe every time we took a step hoping not to trip a booby trap or step on a land mine. I can't remember the other names you mentioned. I remember mainly only last names.

God bless you and your family for such a terrible loss of a loved one. You should be proud of him he served his country well.

God bless you,
Wayne Garrett

July 18, 2001 6:20 PM

Howdy Patti,

Thank you for your kind message.

I doubt that I ever got to meet your brother. I was just a private, a draftee from Western Kansas, stuck out in the field with a M16 and later an M60 with Delta 4/12. We did not know many of the other fellows in the other companies. Also, the turnover was so frequent, so often men in our own company were gone before we even knew their names. Several weeks after the SSGT was killed, I opted to give the Army a few more years for a change of MOS (it is called re-upping to get out of the Infantry), so I made the move from the Infantry to the Engineers and spent the rest of my tour as a jeep driver, draftsman and illustrator near Cu Chi, and later at Lai Kai, near the Cambodian border.

The first 4 months of my tour there, the time with 199th, has had the greatest effect upon me of any experience I have ever known.

9:52 PM

Howdy Again, Patti,

I am writing again this evening because after I visited the pages about your brother, I realize that I had been confused earlier. After visiting the page, I realize that your brother's name was George and he was indeed one of us in the Delta 4/12. I was sent to the field in March and may well have been one of the replacements for the company losses, which included your brother. I will send you the email address of some of the men who may have served with George.

I am so sorry for your family. So many were taken. From the web pages, I realize he was quite an athlete and a fine young man. One of America's finest.

I believe George must have been in the Grady/Andujar platoon because Wayne mentioned that he knew George and then, this morning you mentioned the puppy and the monkey. I do know that Robert has said they had a puppy in their platoon. The puppy liked to play with the monkey, which was the pet of one of the medics.

Keep me posted when you hear anything and let me know about your plans after you have had some time to think about the book project.

Later,
Bob Fromme

July 17, 2001

Hi Patti,

I just got done looking at the memorial to your brother on Clay Crowders web site. I didn't know your brother, but served in Co C, 4/12, 199th in Aug 69 to Aug 70. I will never forget your brother or the many other comrades who died in that horrible war. I wish you and all your family the best.

God Bless,
Larry Spaulding,
Bellevue, Michigan

Patricia,

I didn't know George Farawell because I didn't get to Vietnam until late August of 69. I was assigned to D/4/12 and am a loyal devotee to all that served in that company. It was the highest decorated company in the 199th Light Infantry and I really feel proud to have served with it.

Try looking in the D/4/12 database. You will probably be able to find someone that served with your brother by checking their date's in country beside their names and email addresses. I have gotten in touch with several of my buddies that way.

I wish you the best in your endeavors and hope you find someone to answer some questions that I'm sure he must have for a buddy that he served with.

Thanks for coming to this site; it's the best that us old "redcatchers" could ever hope for.

Sincerely,
Ricky W. Jones
D/4/12 199th LIB 69/70

MY PARENTS

We were just an average American family. My dad was born in Elizabeth NJ the younger of 2 children.

My mother, on the other hand, has an enormous family. She lived on a 114-acre farm in Wilcox, PA with her 10 siblings. They worked the farm for food and dairy products. One by one the kids left home and the responsibilities went to the next oldest. No one finished high school. The boys went into the military. Three of the sisters went to NJ to start a new life including my mother. She lived with friends and cousins to share expenses.

My mother met my dad at work in a paper company. They dated for a short time before Dad had to leave for the service. Mom continued dating while he was gone. His first leave, he bought her an engagement ring.

My dad was a Staff Sergeant in WWII for 4 years but not in combat. He was stationed in Newfoundland. They married in Wilcox. Mom did not have a white wedding gown or big reception, just a soldier in his Army uniform and Mom in a pretty dress with the biggest corsage. My mother was 28 when she married and 32 when she had me.

Housing was made available for veterans in different locations in NJ. They were called veterans homes. Mom and Dad moved in a 2-bedroom unit in Elizabeth, NJ. They had 3 kids. I am the oldest; George was born 15 months after me, and Stephen was born 2 years later. All our neighbors were young veteran couples with children our ages. It was a great neighborhood with 89 kids on our street. Everyone started to move about the same time going in different directions to buy their first house on the GI Bill. We were thrilled with our new house in Linden, which Dad bought for $14,000. I finally had my own bedroom and my brothers shared one upstairs. After moving in, they paved the street in front of our house and built a playground on the corner! That same playground would later be named for George.

Today we reminisce of those carefree, simple days. Everyone seemed to be the same. You did not see who was rich or poor. Mom stayed home had a snack ready when you come home from school. You changed into your play clothes ran out the door until dinner to play with the kids at the playground. Finances were tight and we learned to entertain ourselves. There were no lessons, gymnastics, only sports at school. You had one car in the driveway and one phone with a party line. We ate dinner every night as a family unit.

Our family was very religious. We attended catholic school until 8th grade and Linden High School. During Lent we would pray as a family saying the rosary. We would say "Dad we already said the rosary in school today and went to Mass", he would say "get in here it won't take long as he would light the candles".

When George left for the military my dad almost lived in the church. Candles were lit, rosaries were prayed, novenas were made but prayers were not enough. My parents were beside themselves with worry. I was a wreck. It was the first time in my life I felt out of control.

MY BROTHER

George was born in 1949 and was one of the most beautiful boys you ever saw. He and I had this white hair that made everyone ask us "where did you get that beautiful hair"? And we would say "from God". My dad played semi pro softball and he would take us with him. We loved sitting in the bleachers watching the game and most of all getting all the attention plus soda and ice cream.

George was an ardent sportsman. He excelled in many sports. As long I can remember he always had a ball in his hand, it didn't matter what kind. He could do it all. His favorite when he was young was playing hit the step on the front porch. Every now and then he would miss one and the ball would slam into the storm door sending my dad out yelling to stop that! We were always playing a game of something at the playground, dodge ball, softball, and basketball.

At an early age, George started bowling. He won and many trophies over the years. His room was filled with them. He met most of his friends at Jersey Lanes. The "alleys" is where they met to hang and be together. They worked there, bowled there almost lived there. They had so much fun and were considered a unit. Don't mess with the "guys". George was their protector.

Here are a few stories for your amusement. They decided to make money by valet parking cars at the alleys. One couldn't drive a stick he ripped up 2 lawns. Did I mention some of them did not drive yet? They went to Staten Island where you could drink at 18. They all hung out at Dinino's playing pool, etc. Many a night they drove over the bridge with angels on their shoulders.

In elementary school he played basketball for St. Elizabeth's School CYO team. He played PAL baseball, Linden High School Varsity and Union County baseball in later years. He played third base and pitched. If he was playing, my Dad was in the stands cheering him on.

George and I were very close we even shared a best friend, Richard Gagliardi. Richard was my age in all my classes and homeroom in HS. George had so many friends in so many different places, bowling, sports, school, work, etc. There would always be boys in our house coming and going. They would play poker at our house when they were older. They always had a good time. I always felt George did more in his short life than a lot of people do in a lifetime.

George loved to save money a quality I do not have nor does my brother Stephen. He bought my parents a stereo before he went into the service. We still have it today my mother won't part with it even though it does not work. He loved Roy Orbinson, the Smothers Brothers and Bill Cosby. He bought some comedy albums of Bill Cosby he would play them over and over and laugh at Fat Albert.

My dad, George and me at one of dad's ballgames people would think we were twins.

George and me in 1953, we had the mumps.

George, Stephen and me on Easter Sunday
in our new house in Linden, NJ.

MY WEDDING

I met my husband, Elliott on the first day of my new job after graduating high school in 1965. He is 7 years older than me so I was just a kid when I started there. We worked together for 3 years before we started dating. One night we were all working late at the end of the month. Ell said, "What are you still doing here"? He then said "You want to go to dinner?" Gene who is our best friend to this day, threw his pen up in the air and said "we thought you were blind!" He said he was not blind just waiting for the right time.

We knew this was "it" after our second date in February. When I got engaged in April 1968, I was so excited. We planned a small wedding on Oct 6, 1968.

I had to face, in August of that year, George being drafted and going into the army.

While George was in basic training at Fort Dix, in the summer and fall there was much unrest in Newark, NJ with the rioting in the streets. One weekend he was able to come home he brought 2 guys from the Midwest. Mom made them the greatest dinner and Elliott took them to New York City on Saturday night. What a great time they had. They could not get over the tall skyscrapers, all the lights, old men getting out of limos with their "daughters" and the very hectic pace.

George could not be home for our wedding. He was to be an usher. They were on alert at Ft. Dix. My dad tried everything to get him home to no avail. So he was not in any of our wedding pictures. That broke my heart.

SAYING GOOD BYE

George was home for Christmas and through New Years. It was bittersweet having him home and hanging over our heads was the thought of saying good-bye.

He and Barbara and all the guys had the greatest time on New Years Eve. They all have pictures of that happy night. Rich made a toast to George and the partying ceased to dead silence reminding them of what lay ahead in a few short days.

The saddest day of my life was his last day home and saying good-bye to him when he left for Vietnam. Each one of us spent time alone with George dealing with our emotions. He said simply to me, "I don't want to go". Those words still haunt me. We cried together.

We drove him to the airport where he met other soldiers. It was so sad to see these young boys going off to war. Back then you boarded the plane outside. George was the only one that turned around and waved to us. My mother knew at that moment he was not coming home. It stabbed her heart that wave from her boy.

This is one of my favorite photos and the last one of George and me during Christmas 1968.

BOOK II
THE LETTERS

LETTERS FROM GEORGE

I hope you cherish these letters as I do. I hope they touch your soul. They will remind you how precious life is even on your worst day. Look up to heaven and say a prayer, George will hear you and give you peace.

They are letters sent to me and my husband, Elliott and my Mom and Dad. My Dad and I read them often for comfort. I just read them to my mother recently she had not read them since they came. She could not bear it.

This was my first postcard from Fort Dix in Sept. 1968; he is referring to my wedding in counting the days.

Hi Sis!

How are you doing? I got some free time so I thought I would write you. I got some of your letters. Boy it feels real good to stand in the mail line and get your name called off. So keep them coming. Ok?

You must have about ten calendars and just counting the days. Right? You must be getting nervous. Don't worry about anything going wrong because Ell is all right in my book.

We got our rifles today. (M-14) I took it apart and put it back together already. I had KP last week and it was rough. We all might get it again. I also got another haircut too. Boy, do I have a baldhead.

I miss you all and send my love to all. Well let me go now cause I have to write Mom and Dad.

Love,
George
PS Write soon.

Postcard from Vietnam Jan 1969

Hi sis!

How are you and Ell doing? I'm fine and things are looking brighter. I may get a break and go with the engineers instead of the infantry. I'm still waiting to get into a company. My buddies shipped out yesterday. They are in the 1st Calvary. That's bad.

We had a blast in San Francisco. We did everything. The weather here is about 110 degrees during the day and pretty cool at night.

Well, God bless you and I miss you.

Love,
George

22 Jan 69

Dear Mom and Dad:

How is everything in the house? How are you feeling? I am fine and doing better. It took 19 hrs by plane. We stopped in Alaska and Tokyo. We landed in Ben Hoi and took a bus to Long Binh.

When we got in Long Binh my two buddies had orders and I didn't so I am still here. I feel a little bad because we broke up but that's life. They got a pretty bad infantry unit. There were about 82 infantry men put on guard duty. And I am one of them. This means that we will be here for least 7 more days. Guard duty has 3 hours on and 6 hours off. It isn't that bad at all. Plus the last 2 groups were put into engineering instead of infantry. They were just like me. They were in infantry and didn't have orders so they pulled guard duty. That would really be great if the same happened to me.

We can't get any mail until we get into our own Company. So you can't write until then. I'll write whenever I can. OK?

How is gramps doing? And Stephen? I hope he is being good.

How are the new Enyedys making out? Did they get their car yet? Tell them I'll write as soon as I get a chance.

How is Gags doing? Did he stop over the house yet?

I am at a pretty big base now. You hear mortars every once in awhile. There are thousands of soldiers coming in and out all day. We have Viet Cong ladies working in the mess hall and all over the base. They are so tiny they look like little dolls.

The weather is HOT. Well let me tell you it gets to 100 degrees before noon, then 110 degrees until 3:00. The nights aren't that bad. It gets down to 70.

Did you get my clothes yet? I sent boots and fatigues home from Oakland.

23 Jan 69

Hi: How are you today? I feel good. Just finished taking a shower. I'm going on guard duty in an hour so I thought I would write a few more lines.

The food here is pretty good roast beef and ham. We don't have too much rice.

I got some post cards and will send them out as soon as I can. My money is going fast. It should last until payday. Here the money is paper just like monopoly.

Let me go for now. Love and miss you all.

Love always,
George

---

25 Jan 69

Dear Mom and Dad,

How is everyone doing? I am fine and sorry I couldn't write more letters cause I have to borrow stationery. I don't have any.

I guess I told you that me, Sebold and Kep got split up. They got into a real bad outfit, 1st Calvary.

Today I got off guard duty and found out where I am going. The guy who runs the IBM machines told me that I am going to have it pretty easy. I'm in the 199th Light Infantry division. You would never guess where that is, right here in Long Binh. Long Binh is the biggest base and one of the safest in Vietnam. That's what a lot of people are saying anyway. **This is the biggest break of my life. Except for being in a family like ours that is the biggest thing in my life.**

I met a kid from DC. He was on guard duty with me. He is a real good kid and he is going with me. So at least I know someone. But I'd give anything to have Sebold and Kep with me. We had a lot of good times together. **Boy, I hope they make it cause I know I going to. I can't miss with all of you behind me.**

I might even get to see Ronnie Kisylia here because everyone comes in and goes home from here. This might even be better than engineering. None of the guards got engineering anyway. They all got split up.

The food here is pretty good I think I put on a few pounds. My arms are all sunburned.

I will probably have an address soon. When I get it I will send it you in a hurry. I will probably ship out tomorrow to my company. I can't wait.

How is everybody doing? Tell them all I send my love. When you send me a letter please send me a little wallet calendar. Ok?

How is Gags doing? Boy I wish he were in San Francisco with me. He would never believe the time we had.

Over here we are one day ahead. Today is Saturday. Well let me go for now. I miss and love you all.

Your son,
George

PS Don't forget the calendar. *I have to start counting the days.*

27 Jan 69   This is George's 20th Birthday

Dear Mom and Dad,

How are you all doing? Fine I hope. I'm doing all right. We just started training again. It lasts for 1 week then we go to our company. The training is not bad at all. It is just classes, sitting and listening. We have 1 hour of PT every morning. We get a lot of sleep too. I am well rested. The food here is the best I ever tasted in the army.

I am staying in Long Binh. I know for sure because we got assigned today. My buddy and me I told you about are together. We are Company D4/12. My mailing address is:

PFC George T. Farawell
US 51987070
199th Lt INF Bde, Co D-412
APO San Francisco 96279

That is my mailing address so you can start sending mail anytime. Give it to Gag and everyone else. OK?

Today I got my M16. This is the one I keep for the whole year. It is almost brand new. We also got a lot of equipment. Somebody stole my canteen and pistol belt already. But I get another one when I get to my company. **Delta Company.** So no sweat.

We only had one shot when we came over here. I was surprised. We also started to take malaria pills today. We're supposed to take a big orange one, 1 every week, and a small white one everyday.

The mosquitoes are really big and plentiful here. They issued tent nets. It is a net that you use as your tent in the field. It is really big and works real well. It lets the cool air in and stops the bugs.

I am now Private First Class (PFC). In February I will start making $211 a month, tax-free. All they take out is Social Security and my bond money.

They have soldiers deposit over here. It sounds real good to me. Every month you put your money in and you can't take it out until you go home. It collects the highest interest 10% quarterly. Is that good or what? So I was thinking about putting $100 a month in, keeping $50 for myself and putting the rest in the finance office. The finance office will keep whatever you don't need and add it to next month's paycheck and that continues. If you need money you just go to the finance office and get it. I figure the money I put into finance will help me when I go on R&R. Then if I get some extra money I'll send it home. I hope you understand what I just said. If you do, tell me what you think. Ok?

You can send my camera now and don't forget the calendar too. I can get film and flash bulbs over here cheaper.

We have to get patches sewn on our shirts. The patches are really cool looking. I think I'm going to get a short haircut again. It is easier to keep clean.

You know the phrase it is really quiet around here? During the night once in awhile you may hear mortars. It must be true about this being a safe place.

I met a couple of buddies that I took AIT with in LA. They are training with me now too. I don't know if they will be in my company yet. I'll find out tomorrow. You know this training is for guys in mortars, artillery and the like. You have to take it before you get into your company. We also have some National Guards here that were called up.

I hope you got my letters and post cards. How is everyone doing? What is the weather like?

Patti and Ell got their new car. Boy I'm so proud of her and happy she met the right guy, did she change her job yet? I think she should stay there don't you?

How is big Stephen doing with his girl friends? Is he being a good kid? He better be.

Well tomorrow night I'll write Patti, Gag and Stephen if I have the time like I had tonight. Well its 9:30 and time to get to bed. I can't tell you in words how much I miss you and love you. So let me go for now and God bless all of you.

Your loving son,
George

PS Don't forget my camera and calendar. Write soon. Love you all.

29 Jan 69

Hi Sis!

How are you and Ell doing? Fine I hope. I am fine and putting on some pounds. I'm in the middle of training now.

We have one week of training altogether. It is really simple. All we do is sit and listen all day. In the morning we get up at 5:30 and run a mile. Then we come back and sleep until 7:00. We go for breakfast and have off till 9:00. We have classes till 11:30 am. We also have a half-hour off before dinner and supper. We are off after supper too.

Last night we saw a movie "The Dirty Dozen". They built a screen and put it up in the street in front of my barracks. All the soldiers were on the street watching it. It was real sharp.

The weather here is really hot. I mean it gets close to 100 degrees. The sergeant told us that it is the cool period now too. I'll look like Buckwheat on the little rascals.

We got our weapons yesterday. I keep it for the whole year. (M-16). It is almost brand new.

I bet you I put on at least 15 lbs. The food at the mess hall is great. Barbequed steak, chicken with a red sauce on it and all you can eat too.

My mailing address is on the envelope. If you lose it mommy has it.

How is your job? Did you leave or stay there? How is Ell making out? Did you get the new car yet?

They say the mail takes about 10 days. I am stationed in Long Binh. I think it is southeast of Saigon. It is the biggest base over here.

Well let me go for now I have to write Gag before the movie.

So take care. Love and miss you a lot. God bless you and Ell.

Your loving brother,
G I George
PS Write soon.

31 Jan 69

Dear Mom and Dad,

How are you doing? What is new in Linden? Nothing new over here. I am fine and doing better. Love and miss you all. I got another baldy today. It feels real good. Nice and cool.

My other buddy is going to the same company. So now there are 3 of us going together now. Today we went into the gas chamber. That was really something. They made us take our mask off. My face started to burn and our eyes watered for about 15 minutes.

Tomorrow is our last day of training. We have to cross over the river on a rope and zero our weapons.

We got paid the other day. I got $150. All in paper money even the change is paper. It gets me all confused but I will learn. You know how I am with money. I going to buy a watch, some other things and save the rest.

Well have to go for now time for bed. Love and miss you. Write.

Your loving son,
George
Send a picture of my car. Tell everyone I said hi.

George had a 1957 turquoise 2 door Chevy Impala. It was his pride and joy.

4 Feb 69

Hi! How is everything at home? I am fine. We're out in the field now and have the afternoon off. Monday, Tuesday and this morning we went out in the rice paddies. Boy it was just like one big mud puddle. We didn't get time to change clothes or wash for 2 ½ days. It is sure rough walking through 1 ft of mud and about 3 ft of water with your weapon and 30 lbs of ammo on your back.

So far, we didn't have any contact with Charlie. I hope we never do either. We are out here guarding a bridge and it is not that bad. Every other night we go on an ambush. That is where you sleep. I am averaging about 4 hrs of sleep a day. It is not bothering me though. Here at camp you pull guard when you don't go on an ambush. You get about 3 hrs if you are lucky. We are right by the river so you go for a swim to get clean.

All the guys here are great. They treat me real good. They tell me how to do things and all that stuff. Monday we ran a sweep through the rice paddies for 3,000 meters. Tuesday we pulled off another sweep through rice paddies and a couple of VC villages. We did not see anything but found some VC weapons and field gear.

Listen about once a month please send me some deodorant and other toilet articles. We run out fast out here. Also send me a pair of shorts. You know cut off work pants. OK?

They say that I'll probably be able to write once a week if I am lucky. Sometimes the guys don't write for 2 or 3 weeks. So just keep writing. OK? My letters will probably be short.

Tell everyone I said hello and I was asking for them. Well I have to go now, see you in a little while.

Love and miss you all.
George

PS Just got my first letter, one from you and cards from Patti. Tell Patti thanks and it is good hearing from you.

---

5 Feb 69

Hi Sis!

How are you and Elliott doing? I received your card yesterday and was very happy to hear from you.

It sure is rough out here but I'm too tough to realize it. You should see the way the people live. They clean their food in dirty water! You just wouldn't believe it.

We went out on a couple of sweeps the last four days we have ambushes at night and hardly any sleep. Walking through mud 1 ft. deep and water 2 ft. It isn't like AIT or basic. All work and no play.

The guys here told me that they only get a chance to write maybe once every 2 weeks. So I don't know how often I'll get to write.

We are located 20 miles southwest of Saigon at a bridge. There's a river here where we go to bathe when you get time. This is a great location.

On my way out here Sunday we went through Saigon. That place is worse than New York. The drivers are nuts. They go on the wrong side of the road and cut people off, they just nuts. There is no white line in the middle of the road either. People here drive motorbikes. The ratio is 15 bikes to every car or bus.

Tell Mom and Dad never to send any money cause I'll never be able to cash it in. I forgot to tell them.

Well I have to go in a hurry now so see you soon. Love and miss you.

Love,
George

---

6 Feb 69

Dear Mom and Dad:

How is everything today? I am fine and learning a lot. I'm getting use to the climate here too. The last couple of nights have really been cold. Today we went on a patrol for 4 hrs. It was about 3 miles. All walking. I saw more villages and rice paddies. I also saw Esso and Shell gas stations. Sometimes we see the gas trucks.

We are supposed to move from here Monday. We are moving down the river to relieve another company. They will come up here and we will go down there.

I went on an ambush again last night. We didn't see anything again. You catch a lot of sleep on ambush about 6 or 7 hours. Today while we were going through the village we took a break.

The people come out and look at you. All the little kids come over and talk to you. The kids want food. We couldn't understand them but we did our best. We told them to climb the coconut tree bring us some coconut and we would give them some food. (chop chop) They came back with bananas, coconuts and something else. The fruit was really good.

Little kids come up to you and sell coke for 25 cents. Some of these little kids have a lot of money. My buddy and I had our laundry done for 50 cents. I pick it up today. The kids did a real nice job.

You know I don't wear underwear anymore. They say it is better not to because you get a rash if you do. My buddies are here in the same platoon but different squads. I still see them a lot. We had a party Sunday with beer, soda, potato chips and some other good things. The beer really tasted good. First one I had since San Francisco.

We had a kid drown the other day from my company. He volunteered to go across the canal in a small boat. The boat capsized and I guess he panicked. He was supposed to be a good swimmer. I knew the kid when he came to the company we pulled guard duty. He was only here 3 days. It was really a shame.

How is Stephen doing? Tell him I said Happy Birthday because I don't think I'll be about to write him until later. How are Daddy, Gramps, Aunt Rita and everybody else? How is the dog? Does she know I'm gone?

Mom when you send me deodorant also send me some foot powder too! Enough to last a couple of weeks. Ok? I take my boots off whenever I can get a chance and let them dry out. But I very seldom get a chance. I need some handkerchiefs too. Green ones you get in the army & navy store.

Well let me go for now, I have to start guard duty in the bunker we set up. I love and miss you and will see you in a little while.

Love,
George

PS Tell Patti I got the calendar. Now I can start marking off the days. Thanks.

Good night and sweet dreams.

9 Feb 69

Dear Mom and Dad,

Hi! How is everything? I'm starting to receive your letters and it makes me so happy to read them. I am fine and doing well.

Today we moved from the bridge down the river. We are now on the banks of the river. It looks pretty good here. I just got finished swimming and cleaning my self up.

My friend Glenn and I are in the same bunker. It is a 2 man bunker and real cozy. Glenn bought a little dog for $15. It is so small and is about 6 weeks old. He stays with us except when we go on patrol. We have no name for him yet. He is brown and white with a black nose. He is such cute little thing.

I went on ambush last night and got 6 hrs of sleep. That was really great. We only had 1 hour of watch. The only thing bad about being on the riverbank is we don't get hot meals here. We eat sea rations for breakfast, lunch and dinner.

We went out on patrol yesterday and I really hated it. I just put on clean clothes and we hit water neck high. That was really bad stuff.

Here are some things you can send me: deodorant, candy, toothpaste, shaving cream and razors, writing material and Kool cigarettes. Also some ink pens. Send whatever you can.

Listen don't send me any money. We are not allowed to have American money. If they find you with it you get a court martial offense. Tell Daddy I appreciate him sending the money but I can't cash it in unless I'm in the base camp. Right now we are in the field and will be for a couple of months. So, I am sending the money back and do me a favor and put it in a xmas club and when I get home I will have some extra money. Sorry I could not get any beer with the money Dad but there just isn't too much beer or soda here. When we do get it, it is free.

I have to write on the back of the paper because I am running out of stationery. Send me some fast ok?

The dog just got up so I have to feed him. He eats some of our sea rations. A couple of guys bought monkeys. They have them on chains, and they are so friendly.

How is the weather back home? Tell everybody I miss them very much and that I said hi. I got a card from Aunt Rita with $5 in it. Tell her thank you ok. I will send some post cards when I go in from the field.

Well I have to go for now. I love and miss you.

Love,
George

---

11 Feb 69

Dear Mom and Dad,

How are you doing today? I'm fine and was off this morning so I thought I would write. This letter will be short because I have no paper left.

So far it has been quiet here. We go on patrols everyday and we have one this afternoon at 1:00. Our company will be on TV next week on NBC. They had photographers here taking pictures of us walking through the rice paddies.

I heard on the radio you got a lot of snow. It must really be cold.

In our time off we walk around in our shorts. Wash our clothes and then go for a fast dip in the river. Clean our weapons, etc.

Remember the bridge I told you about? It got hit last night with rockets and mortars. I don't know if anybody got killed but 20 were wounded. Just 2 days after we left it, it gets hit. We lucked out on that one.

My legs are all bit up from the mosquitoes. They are big. My boots are falling apart already. The sole is coming off.

The other day I had to carry the radio. It weighs about 35 lbs. I dropped the receiver in the water. I was lucky I didn't fall in. I don't like carrying it you lose your balance too fast.

Our dog is doing fine. He is awful at night. He sleeps all day.

How are Stephen, Gramps and everybody else doing? How is Stephen doing in school?

Did you see Patti and Ell's new car yet? When are you and Dad getting a new car? I hope before I come home so I can use it until my new Rivera comes in.

Well have to go for now keep writing and keep the faith.

Love and miss you,
George

---

21 Feb 69

Dear Mom and Dad,

How are you all doing? How is the snow? I hear you got a lot of it. I'm sorry I could not write sooner but my company has really been on the move. Really pushin!

We were on the move for 2 weeks in a row. We did not even have a chance bathe. We just came in off a 2-day operation that was HELL!!!!!! Mud and water plus we had no water to drink for 2 days.

Last night we had an ambush patrol and today we are off. Time to write about 6 letters and drink about 10 Buds.

You know nobody knows what Nam is really like until you've been here. **I know I am going to heaven when it is my time (that is not for 90 yrs yet) cause I am in hell now.** You never know how much you appreciate the little things in life back in the states until you miss them. This company has all great guys who do their job when it's time and fool around when it is time to relax. The guys are one big family and it helps make the time go faster.

You never know what day it is unless you look at the calendar or have a calendar watch. Other than that you just count off the days.

This is the biggest experience of my life. Anybody who goes home from here is a full-fledged man. I don't care who he is.

So how is everyone back home? Fine I hope. You and Dad might get a Caprice? It is about time. Did you start that Xmas club for me yet? I hope you did. I have been receiving your mail and Patti's too. You feel so good when you get a letter. It really helps pick you up.

How is Gag doing? I got his letters too. Is Stephen going to that school? I hope he does.

Well 7 more days until pay day. I didn't get a chance to get my money straight yet but this time I will. I'm can really use the 10% interest.

You will never guess what I am doing? Carrying the radio. It isn't that bad because you get out of some stuff. And you don't have to carry anything else except your weapon. It is attaches to a rug-sack and I carry it on my back.

How are Patti and Ell doing? She is really happy and I am so proud of her. I'm glad she is keeping the old job. I hope you can read this but when you don't write for a while your writing gets sloppy. Plus I have nothing to lean on.

One day we built a new bunker. Moved about 5,000 sand bags and other things. That reminds me of working construction. I really did some sweating that day.

Did you get the money I sent back? I didn't get the package yet. I missed a couple of good pictures; I hope the camera comes soon.

Why don't you buy me an album and when I send you my pictures home you put them in the album. Ok. I just don't have the time or enough space to carry it around.

Well keep writing and I miss you all and send my love to you. I am going to go for now. So long.

Your loving son,
George

11Feb 69

Hi Sis!

How are you and Ell making out? I'm fine and have the morning off. This afternoon at 1:00 we have a patrol.

Remember the bridge we just moved from? It got hit last night by Charlie. I don't know if anybody got killed but 20 were wounded. So far it is pretty quiet around our area. I hope it stays that way.

Did I tell you me and my buddy Glenn got a dog? He is about 6 weeks old. He is really playful and is so cute. Everyone plays with him.

The other day I washed my clothes in the river and they came out dirtier than when I started.

How is the new car? Lots of luck with it. Mom and Dad should get one don't you think?

I am receiving all of your mail so far and keep it coming. OK! It really picks me up. I got a letter from Stephen. He says Dad is giving him hell for his grades in school.

My company is going to be on the NBC news either this week or next. They took pictures of us going through the rice paddy. Maybe you will see me on TV.

How are Ell's mother and father doing? Tell them I was asking for them and send my love.

Well I have to get ready for that patrol so keep writing and I'll write whenever I get a chance.

Love,
George
Love and miss all of you.

---

21 Feb 69

Hi Sis!

How are you and Ell doing? How is the new car? I hope everything is fine. I'm fine and I have a day of rest after 14 days of steady moving. I sorry I could not write but we were so busy.

The last 2 weeks I really went through hell and high water. Today I am going to write letters and drink BUDS.

We were on a 2-day operation and didn't have any water for 2 days. Five didn't make it. They had heat exhaustion. A helicopter had to come out and get them. *My pride was the only thing that kept me going.*

I bet Mom and Dad are really worrying? Well they can put their minds to rest I'm well and safe.

Excuse my handwriting cause I'm trying to write 6 letters before I get called for a detail. I hope you can read it.

How is your job? How is Ell doing? I sure hope Mom and Dad get a new car. It's about time, don't you think. They can borrow my Rivera when I'm not using it.

I am glad Aunt Rita is happy with Ann. Ann is a really nice girl. It seems like I miss all the weddings. Aunt Rita is just wonderful. She keeps sending me cards. I'll have to write her.

Everyone is sitting around writing letters and listening to the radio. There is only one channel on the radio. It is really boss it plays all the top tunes.

Our little dog is really getting big. You should see him play with the monkey this kid has. It is really something.

I'm going to get Ronnie K's address from his girl. She wrote to me and said she'll send it as soon as she gets it. I'd really like to hear from him.

Time is flying here. I have been here a month already. You never know what day it is only the date. By the time you know it the weeks fly by.

I am carrying the platoon radio now. It isn't that bad. It keeps me out of a lot of stuff.

Well I am running out of words so I don't know what else to say except take care and I miss you so much.

See you in 11 months.

Love,
George

---

27 Feb 69

Dear Mom and Dad,

How are you doing? Fine I hope. I am okay and having a good time when I am not going through rice paddies. They started to bring beer out here, every Monday we have beer and soda for nothing. So we drink and drink and have a blast after a long day.

I received your 2 packages but where is my camera? I need it! Our base got hit with two rockets the other day. Nobody was hurt. Thank God. We still did not name the dog yet; he is getting big and fat. I washed my clothes and boots today. I have the little kids do them for some e-rations, I cleaned my weapon and now I am going to wash myself.

The cookies were great and thanks for the KOOLS. I can't get any KOOLS here. I was going to write a lot of letters today but I am not in the mood. Maybe later I will write to Patti and Gag.

I got a letter from Ronnie Kisylia yesterday. He is on his way. He does not have an address yet. He has to go through all the stuff I did.

How are Stephen and Daddy doing in bowling?

Well 2 more days until pay day. I am going to stop a minute to eat. Continue later.

---

28 Feb 69

Hi how are you today? I am sorry I didn't finish the letter yesterday but I got into a card game. My 2 buddies and me played blackjack I won $11.

Today we have the day off and it is payday. Please send me some presweetened kool-aid. I put it into my canteen. We get a hot meal for supper, last night we had chicken.

My squad does not have anything tonight so we will drink some BUD. I don't need too much sleep to keep me going. I'm getting use to 6 hrs. a night.

Well I am going to say so long for now. God bless.

Your son,
George

28 Feb 69

Dear Sis:

How are you and Ell doing? I'm fine and just finished writing Mom. You know I have a problem when I write Mom and Dad. I can't think of what to tell them, except that I love then and am doing fine.

We had the last 2 days off and we are just lying around cleaning up and cleaning our weapons. Today is payday. We usually go about 2 weeks of going through rice paddies before getting a day off.

They don't sell beer here until 4 PM so we have to drink soda till then. Then we really go to it.

I got the package Mom sent. I'm still waiting for camera. My buddy Glenn got his so we're getting 2 copies of each picture made up.

I just got a letter from Ronnie K. He has to go through all the stuff that I did. I'm glad Ron and Diane are getting along better. I am waiting for a letter from them.

Yesterday we played some cards with Glenn and some of my buddies. I won $11 playing black jack. Probably will play again later.

Well I have to go for now. I'm receiving all the mail now so keep writing and I will answer as soon as I can.

Your loving brother,
George

1 March 69

Dear Mom and Dad,

How are you today? I'm fine and the Sergeant just inspected my weapon. He said it was really clean.

I got the package with the camera in it yesterday. The only thing wrong is that I can't get film until somebody goes back to the main base in Long Binh. That is not often. So you will have to send me some? Ok? Kodak 126-20. I was thinking Mom maybe you could send some hamburger rolls, a couple of cans of sloppy joe mix, crackers and cheese and some other food. Ok?

Well today is Saturday and the 3rd day off in a row. I just can't believe it. I took a couple of pictures already. I will take it on patrol with me too. This way I can take pictures of the people and their houses. Also some of the canals we have to cross and the rice paddies. It is still hot here. I'm getting a pretty good tan. This morning I washed, shaved and now I feel good. It was the first time I shaved in 2 ½ weeks.

I got paid yesterday and the finance people are coming out today. So I will get things straightened out. I have to find out a couple of things before I put my money in the Soldier Deposit. Like where does the money go if something happens to me? If you get it then I will put the money in it. But I heard it stays in there for a soldier's home. I got $250 in it already.

Are you and Daddy going to get the new car? I sure hope you do. I got a nice letter from Aunt Sue the other day. I forgot to get her address before I threw the envelope away. Can you send it to me? How is Stephen behaving? I hope he isn't going over the Island a lot. He isn't giving you and Dad any trouble is he? How is Gramps doing? Well tell everyone I said hi. Ok.

Let me go for now. I love and miss you all a lot.

Your fighting son,
George

---

5 March 69

Dear Elliott:

How are you doing? I'm fine and in good shape. I'm about 175 lbs now. This place is really bad. Day in and day out in mud and water up to your neck. When I get home I will sure appreciate the little things in life.

The other night our base by the river got mortared. I was really scared. All you can do is run for the bunker and pray. And that is what I did. My brigade has the highest percentage for VD in Nam. So I think I will keep it in my pants until R&R.

The infantry really works you to death. Months at a time you are on the go. Then you finally get a day off and you sleep all day.

I sure hope you get the promotion. I'll be rooting for you.

I have nothing to get off my chest but I will keep you in mind. The only problem I have is writing Mom and Dad. I really don't know what to tell them.

My company doesn't get into too much combat but we do an awful lot of traveling, by foot that is. Our brigade is the only one in Nam that is self-supported. We can go and help another brigade but they can't help us. Crazy isn't it?

How are your parents? I hope they are fine. Tell them I send my love. Well let me go for now because I can't think of anything else to day. I'll probably think of something after I send the letter out. I always do that.

Well I miss and love all of you and God Bless you all.

The main man,
GI George

---

5 March 69

Dear Mom and Dad,

How is everyone doing today? I am fine and weigh about 175 lbs now. How is the weather at home? I bet there is still snow on the ground.

Well I got my camera and took pictures of our 2-day operation we just came off of. My company had to go to Bien Hoa to help the 5/12th element out. We went through the jungle and found 10,000 lbs of VC rice in 2 days, a couple of weapons and mortar rounds. After we got finished with the operation we got on a Landing Craft Machine and went down the Saigon River from Bien Hoa to Long

Binh. In Long Binh we got on trucks and back to Bien Dien Bridge where we met another LCM and came down the river to our own perimeter. We caught the trucks at Long Binh Bridge. A couple of hours after we left there, the bridge got hit with mortars.

The next day our company went out on helicopters. We only swept a couple of clicks (1000 meters to a click). We caught 4 VC going down a little canal. We told them to stop and they wouldn't so we fired over their heads. They finally stopped and a helicopter came and took them away.

So in 3 days time my company found a VC bunker with 10,000 lbs of rice, a weapon and mortar rounds in it, and 4 VC. That's not bad for only 3 days.

Today the rest of the company went on another operation. Me and 2 other guys are pulling LP (Listening Post) across the river from the perimeter. It's not bad. We have all little kids fooling around with us for sodas and food.

I got a letter from Elliott I will probably write him today. How is everyone at home? Anyone get sick from the weather you had?

I was thinking of having slides made up instead of prints. When I get home I will get a slide projector. What do you think slides or prints?

I took out the Soldiers Deposit. I'm putting $125 a month in it. When I make another stripe I will raise it. Right now I got $375 in it.

Glenn and I did not name the dog yet? I think we are going to call him Speedy because he is so slow and clumsy.

Glenn is from VA and his wife is expecting in May. You should see the small jacket he bought for the baby. It has writing on the back along with a picture of Vietnam. It says Souvenir of my Father Vietnam 69 & 70 written on the back. It also has patches on the sleeves it is really nice.

I got a few pictures of the dog, Glenn and me. I also took some pictures from the helicopter looking down. I hope they come out.

Well time to go. Love and miss you all.

Your loving son,
George

PS Send me the envelopes that press closed. The one's you sent me are all sealed already with the weather here.

9 Mar 69

Dear Mom and Dad,

How are you doing today? We have the day off not because it is Sunday but we needed a rest. I haven't heard from you or Patti for about a week.

I'm fine and going into Long Binh today. I have to get my finance papers straight. That means I will be out of the field for a couple of days. Oh by the way I'm stationed in Tan Bau on the riverbank.

I went to Mass today and received communion. The chaplain gave all of us a rosary. It is made of string with a plastic cross. You wear it around your neck.

How is Stephen doing? Did he decide if he is going to that school or not?

I got your package. I really like the peanuts. We eat them when we drink our Bud. Whenever we get a chance. I have to write to the Strupaitis's and thank them for the cookies. They were really good.

I took about 50 or 60 pictures already. Please send me some more color film. The PX runs out so fast and I hate black and white. Send me a couple of rolls.

We sent the dog in for his shots. He gets his shots for free and he will be back after he gets them. We all miss him already.

I got a letter from Ronnie K. and I got his address. He is with the 25th Inf. Div. Here is his address if you and Patti want to write to him.

PFC Ronnie Kisylia
US 51986067
25th S & T BN
25th U INF Div
APO SF 96225

Well I just got a letter from Dad and Patti. So I will say so long for now and God Bless You.

Your loving son,
George

9 Mar 69

Hi Sis:

How are you and Elliott? I guess you are surprised to hear from me. Since you haven't heard from me in about 2 weeks. We have been real busy.

I just read your letter and I wrote Stephen a letter. Let's see what happens. I'll have to write him again. If he wants to learn the hard way like I did, let him go. I'd like to see him try the school anyway. Air conditioning is real good business. Good future too.

Well I am fine and safe. I feel real good except I miss all of you. Time is going fast here. I've been here almost 2 months.

I took about 60 pictures already, some of the land, my buddies and the dog. Only thing is I can't get any color film and I hate black and white film. Can send me some?

The dog is back at Long Binh getting shots. They'll send him back when he is finished. We all miss him already.

I'm in Tan Bau on the riverbank and have to go to Long Binh tonight. I have to go to finance and straighten everything out.

How did Elliott make out with his promotion? I am praying he'll get it? I am very happy for Rosanna tell her I wish her the best of luck.

I received mom's packages the other day. I loved the peanuts she sent. We ate them with the beer.

I got a letter from Ronnie K. the other day. I sent his address in Mom's letter if you want to write him.

The way I feel about this war is. I think it is a foolish war. We're like puppets on a string over here. We can only fire in certain areas and stuff like that. I'm against it all. So is everybody over here. All the GI's want to do is get his year over with.

Well let me go for now. Love and miss you all.

Love,
George

13 March 69

Dear Mom and Dad,

How are you today? I'm fine and safe. Just got through swimming in the river. Now I'm drying off having a beer. I thought I would drop you a few lines before chow, to let you know what is going on.

Yesterday, we had 4 of my buddies hurt by land mines. They got shrapnel wounds of legs and arms. I saw 2 of them blow up on them. It sure was a terrible feeling.

Everyone was mad because none of the people would tell us where the VC or land mines were? So we just burned down a couple of houses and haystacks. Five houses to be exact!

We figured we could play just like the VC charley does. The people are afraid of what the VC would do to them if they told. Now we'll make them afraid of us too. Some of the people who talk to you during the day are the enemy at night.

I don't know if I told you about Glenn. My buddy is from VA and his wife is having a baby the end of April or beginning of May.

Well tell everyone I send my love and miss them a lot. Time to go to chow. I can't afford to miss a meal over here.

God bless you all.
Your loving son
George

15 Mar 69

Hi Sis:

How are you and Ell doing? I am fine and safe. It rains here in the morning for a few minutes everyday. Pretty soon the rainy season will be here, then 4 or 5 months of rain.

Just got finished writing Stephen a letter. Tried to tell him to at least give the school a chance. Let's see what happens. I hope he goes.

My buddy Glenn's wife is expecting at the end of April. When is Rosanna due?

We have the morning off and got a patrol this afternoon. We just got a new Lieutenant for our platoon leader. He seems like a nice guy, kind of quiet though.

Our little dog is still getting his shots. I hope he comes back soon. We all miss him. We named him Bien.

I just got a package and some letters from you and Mom so let me say so long for now.

Love,
George
Miss and love you.

This is the last letter to my mom and dad. He stepped on a land mine and died on March 18, 1968.

---

16 Mach 69

Dear Mom and Dad,

How are you doing today? I'm fine and safe but am a little upset. It has been a very sad weekend. Two more of my buddies got hurt on land mines.

One of them was Glenn! The other guy was from TN. All three of us hung around together. The doctor said he probably had a couple of broken bones in his right leg. Both of his feet were messed up pretty bad. He won't be back in the field. He will probably get a job in the rear after 4 or 5 months in Japan or the Philippines. The other kid Fred was only hurt a little. He had a cut in the face and arm.

We just finished with a Saturday afternoon platoon patrol. We were walking on the dike toward the river where we were supposed to catch the boat. We started to walk on the road alongside the river. The Lieutenant didn't know where the river was. He thought the road ran into it. I was wondering where we were going. Then all of a sudden POW, and there were Glenn and Fred.

Glenn was always the first man or point man. He was walking point ever since we came out here. He was really good at seeing things and loved to do it. He carried a mine detector. This detector picks up any land mines or any little piece of metal. He turned it off when he got to the road. I guess he thought that nobody would land mine the road. The traps were on the side of the road. He was just careless once.

When I saw Glenn lying there I went over to help. I helped the doctor bandage him and kept talking to him to trying to calm him down. He was really in pain. In about 15 minutes the helicopter came and took him to the Saigon hospital.

That really took a lot out of me because both of us had a lot of fun when we were off. We were pretty close friends for the short time we knew each other. I know we will see each other again though.

We left our sign in the village that was close by though. We all had to burn some houses down. So we burned down 2 old houses.

Well that is it and you know how I feel. I'll probably forget about it after a while but right now everybody has a case of the ass. That is 6 guys in 3 days.

Well enough of that how is the weather? It will start raining here soon. The rainy season lasts for about 4 or 5 months, it starts in April.

I received another package the other day. THANK YOU.

Later I have to get washed up and shave. I haven't shaved in over a month. I am going to try and grow a mustache. I am listening to a basketball game on the radio. Tell Dad Wayne Huckel is playing. I am also eating your Fritos and having a Pepsi.

Well tell everyone I am fine and send my love. Ok. How is Gag doing? Does he come over much? How is Stephen? I wrote him a letter the other day.

Well time to say so long for now. Love and miss you all.

Your son,
George

PS Write soon. Send things you can eat while drinking beer or soda. Ok?

This is George's last letter to my husband.

March 16, 1969

Dear Ell:

What's happening? How is my sister treating you? I'm fine but got the case of the ass. Everyone in my platoon feels the same way.

We lost 6 good men in the last 3 days, all on booby-traps. They are all alive and resting in the hospital. Most of them have big wounds.

One was my buddy Glenn. You probably heard Patti talk about him. Well his legs are pretty bad, his feet too. The doctor said he had a couple of broken bones in his right leg. He will never be back out here. He'll be in Japan or the Philippines for 4 months. Then he probably will get a job in the rear. I'm really going to miss him. We were having a ball on our time off.

Everybody is so mad cause of losing these guys that every time we go through a village we burn it down. I'll tell you what if we run into the VC they better have the person they believe in behind them. Cause we will bring smoke on their poor little ass.

My mother got a letter explaining how it all happened. So if you and Patti want to know more see her. OK?

I'll tell you it really takes a lot out of you when you see your buddy lying there messed up and in agony. Knowing that you can't find the little bastard who put the booby trap there. Well that is what it is like. HELL! You don't know who the enemy is.

Well, how is your new car? You get the dent fixed yet? You get your promotion? Good luck I hope you get it.

Well let me go for now I just wanted to tell somebody how I feel about this whole thing, in my own words. Get it off my chest. It should help me forget easier. Thanks for listening. Take care and God bless.

The Main Man,
George

PS How are your mother and father doing? Tell them I send my love, OK.

I wrote to George everyday even if only a few lines. This is my last letter to George on which came back unopened.

March 17, 1969

Dear George,

I have good news for you-brother. You are going to be an uncle!!! Yes you are. I went to the doctor today and he confirmed the good news. Mom went with me and the both of us were so excited. I took off from work today - went to the doctor- did my food shopping and 4 loads of wash. I am exhausted. The doctor gave me vitamins because I am so tired. He told me the reason - the baby is just starting to form and taking all of my iron and calcium, which is making me, so tired. He also gave me pills for the nausea, which I have in the morning and sometimes at night.

Anyway, the big day is November 3 or the first week in Nov. We would love to have you be Godfather, as I told you before. Once we find out when you are coming home - Ell and I will go to the priest and see if we can hold off the Christening until you come home.

Can you really believe I am going to be a mommy? I can't even believe I am married yet. I suppose the months will drag cause I am so excited already.

Now we have 2 reasons to be really looking forward to the end of the year, you coming home and a new baby.

So - God daddy (where did I get that) take care and I love you so much. I will write again tomorrow when I am a bit calmer.

God Bless You!

Love, Mommy E xxxxxxxooooooo

A few notes for you.

- We never got his camera or pictures that he was so excited to take. They sent us his boots in a box.
- Ronnie requested to bring George home. By the time, they paperwork went through he was home already. In all that time, they were only 7 miles apart from each other. Ronnie did make it home. Thank God.
- I am still looking for **Glenn, Sebold, Kep, Fred, and Dan.** I hope you all survived and have a happy life.
- My dad planned on having the Rivera parked in the driveway when George came home.
- Mom and Dad did get their first new car.
- You can reach me at: Email: penyedy@yahoo.com

THE NEWS

The following sequence of events is uncanny. Angels were present in our house.

We were notified of his George's death on March 19th, my mother was not home. She was getting a box ready to send to him for Easter. She went uptown to buy more goodies. The neighbors saw the Military vehicle and the officers ringing the doorbell. They knew immediately this was bad. They approached the officers; they wanted to know where my dad worked. They went to tell my dad at work and brought him home. When mom pulled in the driveway, the neighbors ran over and told her the Military was there. She ran screaming into the house. She knew immediately her worse fear was realized. My dad and the officers found her crying on the bed. My dad said, "He's gone". She did not want to hear that about her boy.

In March 1968, I was feeling queasy. I went to the doctor and found out I was pregnant on **3/17/69**. **George died on March 18th.** My parents called my in-laws and they called our office to tell my husband Elliott. Ell had to tell me this after work. Can you imagine how difficult that was? The first thing he said was "Think about the baby". For all of us, just finding out I was going to have a baby, the first grandchild, from experiencing extreme joy to extreme grief; I have not experienced anything like that since. It was God's will that I did not lose the baby in the following months. I was sick the whole pregnancy.

It took quite awhile for George's body to come home. The following day we had to go to the cemetery and florist. I have to tell you I don't remember much of the days that followed. It is a blur. I know we all had to buy black dresses. There were endless visits from family and friends. People did everything for us bringing food, making phone calls, etc. We were numb.

The guys were all devastated when they heard George was killed. One by one they came.

A US Army Soldier Honor Guard, named Dan accompanied George's body home. He stayed with us until George was buried. I am ashamed to say we lost contact with Dan as the years went by. Eddie just told me recently that Dan said he never knew anyone so powerful and loved in all of his life.

BALLPLAYER VIET VICTIM

MINE KILLS LINDEN GI

Linden - Army PFC George Farawell, 20, of 723 Bergen Ave., a former high school and recreation league baseball player was fatally injured on March 18, by a mine explosion in Vietnam the Defense Department announced today. He was the son of Mr. and Mrs. George J. Farawell.

Farawell played third base and pitched two years on the starting varsity team at Linden High School where he graduated in 1966.

In 1965 he pitched with the Betsytown Post 1862 VFW team that won the intra county baseball championship.

Farawell also played in the PAL baseball, basketball, and on CYO teams. During 1967, he played baseball with the Elizabeth Colonials in the Union County Twilight League.

Farawell worked for about one year as a carpenter and electrician for Linden Exhibits, before entering the service in August. He was sent to Vietnam in January as a rifleman with the 199th Brigade of the 12 Infantry.

He was a communicate of St. Elizabeth's R.C. Church of Linden, where he served as an altar boy. He was born in Elizabeth.

Surviving is a brother Stephen at home, a sister, Mrs. Patricia Enyedy of Iselin: and his paternal grandfather, George M. Farawell of Linden.

Arrangements are by the Lee Funeral Home, 301 E. Blanke Street.

REFLECTIONS OF A MOTHER

**My mother has had this poem for years
and wanted to include it.**

We did not see you close your eyes,
We did not see you die,
All we knew was that you were gone,
Without a last goodbye.

It was a sudden parting,
Too bitter to forget,
Only those who loved you,
Are the ones who will never forget?

The happy hours we once enjoyed,
How sweet their memory still,
But death has left a vacant place,
This world can never fill.

Your life was one of kindly deeds,
A helping hand for other's needs,
Sincere and true in heart and mind,
Beautiful memories left behind.
Author Unknown

THE FUNERAL

The viewing and funeral were unreal. Flowers filled the rooms. Flowers were shaped into a baseball, glove, hearts, basketball, bowling ball, an American flag, and a rosary. The site took your breath away. No one had to speak, we could not speak, and only sadness took us over. I think everyone in Linden came or sent us a card or letter. We received letters from people we did not know. People who lost sons, brothers, family members in other wars and well as Vietnam.

We had a closed casket with the United States flag draped over it with George's army portrait. We did not see George again; my uncle identified him. He said we should remember him as he was.

With all of our family and friends so devastated we decided on a Military Burial. No one could have been a pallbearer that day.

**James Hayden who was a classmate of mine read
the following poem at the funeral Mass.**

"TRY TO UNDERSTAND"

"I'll lend you for a little time a son of mine, He said,
For you to love while he lives, and mourns for when he's dead.
It may take two or three short years or twenty-two or three
But will you not till I call for him, take care of him for me?
He'll bring his charms to gladden you, and should his stay be brief
You'll have his lovely memories as solace for your grief.
I cannot promise that he will stay, since all from earth return,
But there are lessons taught down there I want this son to learn
I've looked this wide world over in my search for teachers true,
And from the throngs that crowd life's lanes,
I have selected you.
Now will you give him all your love, nor think the labor vain,
Nor hate Me when I come to call to take him back again?
I fancied that I heard them say, "Dear Lord, Thy will be done".
For all the joys thy son shall bring, the risk of grief we'll run.
We'll shelter him with tenderness, we'll love him while we may,
And for the happiness we've known, forever-grateful stay.
But should the angels call for him sooner than we've planned,
We'll brave the bitter grief that comes and try to understand".

Author Unknown

The cars were lined up for miles in the funeral procession after
Mass to the cemetery. It started to rain lightly. At the cemetery taps
were played and the 21-gun salute brought gasps of pain and grief.
The flag was presented to my mother. We had a luncheon at the
Knights of Columbus afterward. I don't remember much of that we
were in a daze.

BOOK III
REFLECTIONS

PFC GEORGE T. FARAWELL MEMORIAL PARK

George's best friend Richard (Gag) in his letters, worked diligently to have our playground dedicated in his memory. Over 600 people attended the dedication.

Col. James Creekman Deputy Chief Of Staff, Army Electronics Command, at Fort Monmouth, NJ presented George's medals to my parents.

The park where we played as kids was now named PFC George T. Farawell Memorial Park in Linden. Richard handled everything. Friends of George's collected donations for the memorial monument, flagpole, and veterans organizations and individual citizens laid nine wreaths on the monument. The Carteret American Legion Band played Taps and the Linden Civic War Veterans served as honor guards.

A reception followed for 350 people.

My grief stricken parents being awarded George's medals.

MY BOY

Of course I had a baby boy on October 31, 1969. There was never a doubt that it was not a boy. We debated over naming him George but at the time it was just too soon. He was the only boy born in the hospital that Halloween day. This baby we longed for was finally here.

I went over as much as I could to see Nanny and Pops. My dad could always be found walking the baby in the carriage, stroller, and in later years his fire truck. My dad had a mop pole and once Elliott got tired with the pedals, Pops would take over pushing him home. Along the way all the little kids in the neighborhood would follow him. Dad looked like the Pipe Piper. When the guys played baseball and I was there, you would find dad in the stands with the baby!

As Elliott got older he spent a lot of time with his grandparents. He would go and not want to come home. He filled the void in their life. My dad had a ritual, they would go to the cemetery Elliott would fill the water cup and put the flowers in. They would stop for hot dogs at the vendor and a pony ride. When he was older they would hit golf balls at the driving range.

ANOTHER DEATH

My dad battled colon cancer for 2 years. He had surgery with a colostomy and later a tumor on his hip so he could not walk. He died at age 57 in 1974. His last words were "Tell Elliott I love him". He was in a coma all day so for him to speak was a miracle.

Another funeral and he was buried with his beloved son. The wake and viewing were the same with family and friends.

My dad would read George's letters over and over for comfort. Mom met Mrs. Schlicker whose son is buried by my Dad at the cemetery one day. Her son Richie went to school with me. He was killed while home on leave. She told mom how my dad would just cry and cry when he was there. He never got over the death of his son. My son missed his Pops terribly after his death.

Another sad day in my life was waving good-by to my mother after the funeral that night. She was standing alone on the front porch with our dog, Taffy. It took my breath away.

As Elliott grew up he had so many of his uncle's traits his love of sports, music, family, and his friends. I always felt my brother was living in my son. He even had the blonde hair his uncle had which darkened up when he got older.

He had so many friends we always had the boys in and out of our house. We use to say how many are up in his room today? He was a drummer, which meant the band always practiced at our house. Even when he went to college the boys would stop over to see us and take a swim. Some of them were in his wedding and they still see each other with their kids. I know George would have been the same way with his friends had he lived.

I don't know if my son ever realized just how he saved all of us from a deep depression since he did not know my brother, or realize how much he is like his uncle. Even to point of liking Budweiser!!! My son is known as the Bud Man. He is so funny, loyal and a devoted husband and father. I am so proud of him as I was of my brother.

CHANGES IN 1998

In 1998 my life changed dramatically. After back surgery I was now home and would not return to work. We decided to move to PA and build our retirement house. We found 3 wooded acres on top of a mountain with many of my relatives 2 miles away.

The best time of the day for me is the quiet morning with coffee. I open the blinds look out at the woods, feed the birds, squirrels plus the deer start coming for their apples. Ell and I have always spent this time of the day to talk and catch up.

I am now caregiver to my mother. She moved in with my husband and me. She has macular degeneration, which is loss of her central vision. She lived on her own with her sister until she was 83. She did not like giving up her independence but she could no longer drive etc.

I often look at her in amazement and wonder how did you get through all of it, the death of her son and 4 years later your husband. My dad was sick for 2 years with cancer before he died. People would say to me I could never do it! Well do we have a choice? You roll up your sleeves and deal with the hand you are dealt.

Mom is a very religious person and she did change some of her habits. She went out everyday no matter what. She kept active and she was always willing to baby sit for me in a heartbeat and the kids never wanted to come home. She had a part-time job for a while which got her out of the house.

1999

Richie Gag made a private vow to himself that whenever he was in the neighborhood he would ride by the park and check on it. What he saw broke his heart in August 1999. The monument had been toppled over and vandalized. He knew what he had to do - fix it. Capt. Don Struck, who was with Richard when he saw the damage, pledged that with the help of the firefighters, they would get it fixed.

Firefighters demolished the base, which was carted off by the city and arranged to get the bronze plaque cleaned before reattaching it. Vincent Gagliardi, Rich's nephew, designed the plans for the new base. Firemen's Mutual Benevolent Association Local 34 in Linden provided about $1,850 in donations including money raised from the union's cheese-steak sale at the city's Cultural Fair in October. FMBA Local 234 Officer's Association contributed $250 more.

Capt. Struck's brother Ray a professional granite installer, donated four days of his own time to install the new $1300 granite base, which is expected to hold up to vandalism. Ray Price from the city Recreation Department created a new sign and arranged for a wood-chip border around the monument base.

In November the Sunday after Thanksgiving, Richard called telling us that George's monument was vandalized. He told us he went to visit George and found it damaged. He was sick at the idea that anyone would do such a thing. The good news was all the repairs were completed. Richard called and the only thing for us to do was attend the rededication on December 12, 1999.

So 30 years later, we met again to rededicate the park to my brother. My dad was missing this time. It hurt as much as it did before. The tears flowed. I wrote a wonderful speech my daughter Amanda had to deliver to everyone at the very last minute. I just could not do it. The day before we buried my favorite Aunt Sue who was my second mother and George's godmother.

Thank you did not seem enough to say to all of them. But that is all they wanted in return. They wanted to help their fellow firefighter remember his friend. I told them I wish each of them a "true friendship" like Rich and George. One that will last a lifetime, even if one is gone in body; he lives on in our spirit.

My mother lost most of her vision in her good eye shortly after the rededication.

My only regret is we did not have all his friends there with us.

**Richard is working on the new monument
with his fellow firemen.**

The Firemen are unveiling the new monument.

2001

My mom is now 86. She is seeing very little. She listens to books on audiocassettes. We try to keep her busy. It saddens me to see her on a daily basis losing her spark and that twinkle in her eye. She is getting frail and slowing down. Life is now an effort. I know I will be losing her soon but she will finally see her boy and her husband again. And grief will visit me again.

Stephen visits a few times a month. He is starting his life over at 50. In retrospect, my brother Stephen had it the hardest. Being a senior in HS and losing his best friend was very difficult.

Those were big boots to fill in his brother's shadow his whole life. Stephen never complained he just loved his brother. He is very easy going to a fault. Life has been tough on Stephen and through it all he is now finding his spirit. He is walking everyday and meditating. He is finding joy in my mother in being able to spend more time with her in the last years of her life. She perks up as soon as he comes in with his laundry!

FINDING EACH OTHER AGAIN

I was reading George's letters recently and thought no one else has ever read these. I wanted to share them with family and friends. What happened to all of his friends?

Richard and his wife Jennifer were visiting for the weekend in June of this year. He and Jennifer read George's letters. The profound effect they had on them renewed my desire to get them published.

George touched so many people. Besides being a loving son and brother, he was a loving friend. He was very strong and protective of everyone he loved. His friends will vouch for that. I feel he is pulling us together again to touch each other in the last miles of our journey in life to explore our hidden emotions that have been buried for years. Heartache we did not deal with at the time it was just too painful and we were just too young.

After the funeral we all went our separate ways. Two of the guys were in the service Ronnie in Vietnam, 7 miles from where George was and Richie Burke in Korea. We never all got together and talked about what happened and how it affected our lives.

A few months ago I went on the website classmates.com, I check my class every so often to see new names. A familiar name appeared on the screen, Eddie Malinowsky our dear friend and neighbor! I immediately sent him an email.

The next day I received an email telling me he just went to the Vietnam Memorial in NJ that same week to **"visit George"**. He had company that night and they were asking him if he ever heard from the family. He said no. The next day there was an email from me after all these years saying hello. He could not believe it! We now keep in touch.

My brother had someone special at the time he left. Who knows what would have happened had he lived. I know they had a wonderful New Years Eve together with all of their friends. Barbara found me in July of 1992; I received a note telling me about a plaque that was presented to Linden High School with George's name on it. The National Honor Society had gone on a trip to Washington DC and visited the Vietnam Memorial. They found George's name and one other soldier from Linden. They scratched his name onto paper, and created a plaque. It is hung in Linden High School. We have kept in touch since then.

I emailed her telling her I am going to publish George's letters and she contacted Ronnie Kisylia. They have not spoken in 30 years. Ronnie is mentioned in the letters. Ronnie was so surprised to hear from her and he just went to the Vietnam Memorial in NJ that past weekend to **"visit George"**. Both were speechless.

I decided I would try and find everyone. It was not that difficult since most of them are still in NJ. I found them one at a time. Once the shock wore off and the tears stopped flowing they were so pleased with what I intended to do. One led me to another. They were all eager to talk about emotions that have been buried for 32 years. I wanted to know how they all found out, what happened in their life.

So we met one Saturday afternoon at George's Park August 11, 2001. We took pictures and went to the alleys to reflect and have dinner. It was quiet, private and all of our emotions flowed from one story to another. You know this was hard on me because I still think of them as 19 like my brother. I had to get a grip on reality. I met all these wonderful men and women who never forgot their friend. They all **"visit George"** at the "Park", the DC Memorial, or the NJ memorial.

They have written a **"reflection of their friend"** 32 years later. They are priceless just like their friend's letters.

**Sam Iacobone, Ricky Kisylia, Mike Favor,
Steve Di Gangi and Ronnie Kisylia.**

Front left: Barbara Lyons Pawlowski, Jennifer Gagliardi, Me, Joyce Colletti Soltis, Richard Gagliardi, Elliott Enyedy, Eddie Malinowsky, Stephen Farawell, Ricky Kisylia, Mike Favor, and Ronnie Kisylia.

REFLECTIONS OF MY BROTHER

At Linden High School in 1968, there was much unrest in school. The Newark riots triggered racial unrest even in our school. There were days they closed the school.

My sister, Patti got married in Oct. 1968 and my brother George was in Fort Dix at the time. He was supposed to be in the wedding. He could not come home because they were on alert. My dad tried everything to get him home for that special day. Now is retrospect we should have just gone down and put him in the car. In those days, you never wanted to get in trouble.

As a senior in HS, the saddest day of my life, I got home one day and the shades were down. I walked through the kitchen and into the living room where my dad met me. Mom was in the bedroom they were both crying. Dad said, "He's gone". I immediately looked at the stereo at his picture, which was face down. The worst has happened and we had no control over it. My brother was gone forever in body because his spirit will live on in me forever until I meet him in heaven.

As a matter of fact he is standing at the gate right now waiting for me (and all of us). Dad has probably got his ear about baseball. George is sitting with a Bud in his hand telling Dad to give it a rest already.

Thinking back now the days that followed I was in a daze at the wake and funeral. It hit me leaving the cemetery knowing I could never again give him a hug, talk to him or just hang out.

I have to live the rest of my life without my brother who I always looked to for guidance. I could never in my whole life be able to fill his shoes. Everyone has great things to say about him, which fills me with happiness. We shared a bedroom and I could never go back there. I hope I can live up to his expectations but that would be impossible.

I miss him to this day so much.

Stephen

REFLECTIONS OF MY FRIEND

July 10, 2001

Trying to put into words what George Farawell meant to me or the impact he had on my life is very difficult for me...but I'll try.

When I first met George and Patti Farawell we were very young. George was one of many friends I had that hung out with us at 4th Ward Park. Patti, George's sister, was also my friend that I danced with at park dances and also built a friendship with as close as George's.

Life was innocent then. Healthy parents, great town to grow up in, strong friendships and only positive thoughts about life and the future occupied our minds.

When George came to Soehl Junior High after finishing up at St. Elizabeth's Grammar School, our friendship started to evolve into much more than casual friends from the park. Our mutual love for sports and life in general made us inseparable. Our peers in Linden would think of George and me almost as one and the same person.

The most fun we had was between the ages of 16 and 18. Our many trips to Staten Island, our many nights hangin' at Jersey Lanes and the many friends I met at the "alleys" through George are memories imbedded in my mind forever.

When George got drafted, it only seemed like a little bump in life's journey only to be continued when his tour in the Army was completed. At the time, I didn't think it was going to be a life altering experience for his family and friends.

When his Basic Training was completed at Fort Dix, New Jersey he mentioned to me that there was a good chance he was going to Fort Polk, Louisiana for Advanced Infantry Training. When he completed that training, it didn't seem long before we all found out he was being sent to Vietnam via San Francisco.

I can honestly say that George did not want to go. Not because George was in any way weak mentally or physically, but because he truly believed he was not coming home! He told me so in his Mom and Dad's kitchen the very day he was leaving for San Francisco.

I am going to skip now to the day we all found out the terrible news about George...

I was stopped on Elizabeth Avenue by a mutual friend of ours named Joe Mazza. I was working for the City of Linden's Engineering Department at the time. Joe said he had just heard a rumor that George was killed in Nam. It is a very difficult thing to express my emotions from that moment until I was sent home from work and went to the Farawell's house to learn the tragic news.

The next few weeks were the most difficult ones in my life. I've since then lost a father, father-in-law, mother-in-law and others that were close to me since then, but we were all so young and naive to life and it's awful experiences at that time and George was so full of life that it was almost impossible to think about life ahead without George being part of it. Needless to say, George's death broke my heart and spirit. And in some ways changed me as a person. I still made people laugh and my life went on, but I can truthfully say it was not the same.

I knew after the very emotional funeral that I had to do something for George. Near his home on Bergen Avenue was a playground. I thought renaming it after George would be an honor for him and his family. With much help from Woyt's Tavern Softball Team, which George and I both played on, and also the Jersey Lane friends... donations and 50/50 raffles were secured to finance the dedication of the park in September of 1969. It was a wonderful tribute to George and I'm sure a very emotional experience for his family.

I was appointed to the Linden Fire Department on December 1, 1971, and on occasion I would take a ride past the park to just think of George. Much to my dismay while riding past the park early in the year of 1999 I found, that due to age and vandalism, the monument and memorial had deteriorated. With the help of the Linden Fire Department the memorial was rebuilt and beautifully redone for a rededication in December of 1999. I know the rededication would be very hard on George's family, but I believe that he deserved another tribute and the ceremony was worth any emotional feelings that it may have brought.

I miss George to this day. For those that knew him, he touched their lives in a way that they will never forget him. For those that didn't know him, let me just say that George was a loyal, trusting friend and a loving son and brother.

I wish George could have met my wife, Jennifer, and to have been there for the birth of my daughter, Natalie, whom he would have been Godfather to. I know he would have loved both of them. I could go on and on but words truly can't express how I feel.

Just a note to George...My life has had a void in it for 32 years now. I know you are in heaven. That is a definite. I was devastated by your death. Someday, we will meet again. Just remember I've never stopped loving you or missing you.

Love,
Richie Gags

March 2, 2016

I didn't know George at the time of his death. Though I came to find out much later that he was the best friend of my husband, Rich Gagliardi.

However, I knew of George years prior to meeting Rich. I remember being about 14 or so and my Mom coming home from work and telling me that one of her coworkers, Mary Farawell, had just received news that her son was killed in Vietnam. I could only think of how close it was hitting home now, as I had never known anyone who died in Vietnam. It touched me greatly and scared me to death.

It wasn't until years later when I met Rich in 1975 that I came to find out that George was his best friend. I, too, had lost a very close friend on the very same day that George died. It was very easy for me to relate to his pain. Since then, I have gotten to know George's Mom, sister, brother and other family members.

Through the power of friendship a park in Linden, New Jersey was dedicated in George's name. I was not there for the dedication of the Park, but had heard the entire story of how it came to be. I was in awe of it all and admired my husband greatly for this undying love for his dear and best friend, George.

Throughout the years, George's name has been spoken many times in our household. We often talk about and wonder how things would have been different in our lives had he made it home. He is sorely missed and I feel a great loss not having known him.

In December 1999, Rich and the hard work of the Linden Fire Department made a rededication of the George T. Farawell Park in Linden, New Jersey possible. I was happy to be there for this one. I could only think of how strong Rich and George's friendship had to be. It amazed me to think that after 30 years he was still that close to Rich's heart. What a wonderful friend George has! It will be a happy day when they meet again.

I can only say that I also admire Patti, George's sister, for putting this book together. I'm sure it has drudged up a lot of mixed emotions for her. But I know all too well it was a labor of love. Thank you Patti for reminding others that men like your brother George is not ever forgotten.

Love,
Jennifer

July 26, 2001

Pat:

George and I decided to boost our draft sometime in late 1967. I remember talking about it in Staten Island one night. We both knew that sooner or later we were going to be drafted; everyone around us was going at that time. He said lets go and get it over with the sooner we go the sooner we come home. Not too much later we received our notice and we were going into the Army. It was August 1968. I remember leaving Elizabeth on our way to Newark to be sworn in and then on to Fort Dix, NJ. We sat next to each other on the bus all the way. It wasn't bad because all of us on the bus were from Elizabeth or Linden so we knew just about everyone.

George and I both took basic training together; we were in the same barracks and the same platoon. I remember coming home maybe twice while at Dix and going to Staten Island with our baldheads. After graduating from basic sometime in late Oct or early Nov. we were walking to the mess hall and that when we got split up. I don't remember how or why but I remember that!

Pat it has been a long time, over 30 years. A lot of what I am writing went through my mind after George was killed in action but this is the first time I ever sat and wrote about my buddy and me. I have to stop once in awhile because tears are coming to my eyes. I often think about what he would be doing now? I know we would still be friends. Things he and I did together growing up we could never forget. The last part of this letter is going to be tough on me.

George and I left for Vietnam on different days. I don't remember how he got my address or how I got his over there. Maybe only after weeks we wrote to each other. Mail was slow there. I remember writing about Barbara Lyons. We only wrote about 3 letters. In one we talked about going to Australia together on R&R. In another agreed to we set up a date because you had to have 6 months in country to go on R&R. I never received another letter from him and before I could write back I received the bad news.

I went to Long Binh to surprise him. I found his company and that was how I found out what happened. Then my mother wrote and told me also. All I thought about after that was I am never going to make it home. I still have 10 months to go. By the time the Army answered my request to come home with George he was back in Linden.

I lost all of my personal belongings one day when my base camp was hit with mortar fire. They hit an ammo dump not far from where I used to sleep when in the rear and all was burned. I was in the field when that happened only for a few days, which turned out to be about 30. That is how the Army worked.

I can tell you much more when I see you. Call me anytime.

Love you and your family,
Ronnie Kisylia

July 29, 2001

Patti,

I am sitting at Merdies tavern writing this reflection. I just walked outside and looked down Bower St. I said hello to George. I tend bar 2 nights a week at Merdies. I try to say hello to George every week. After seeing Steve (your brother) today I will make it a point to say hello every week. Merdies, if you forgot, is on the corner of Elizabeth Ave. and Bower St.

Steve left me with your book. I just finished reading it. The book just reinforced my feelings for life. Life is a gift that can be taken away in a heartbeat.

I think of George often and always-wonder why him and not me. I was the lucky one, I went to Korea, and George went to Nam. I was in Korea when George was killed. I came into my barracks and there was a letter on my bunk. The letter was from Steve Di Gangi. I didn't receive many letters but Steve was good for a letter a month. Steve's letters would ramble on and on which I loved. I opened this letter and a chill immediately went down my spine. I knew something was wrong. Steve's letter was one paragraph.

"Rich I am sorry to have to be the one to tell you that George Farawell was killed in Vietnam." I don't recall the rest of the paragraph. In fact, I don't remember much of that night.

The next day I received a letter from my mother. She sent me a copy of the daily journal, which included the article relating to George's death. My mother's letter went on as follows; "my dear Richard, when I opened the newspaper and saw the picture I said, oh my god it's Richard. I read on and saw that it was George and said to myself, it's just as bad."

It still bothers me a lot about George. Maybe I'm being selfish, I don't know. I can't help but wonder why him and not me.

I carried George's picture in my wallet for many years. Now it's in my nightstand. I have a lot of great memories of George; I just wish I had more.

Sincerely,
Richard Burke

July 25, 2001

Patti:

I would love to write something for your book & reflect on your brother George.

Being back from the Nam only a short time, George was home getting ready to go to the Nam. I remember the night before he left I was at your home at the time I didn't talk much if at all about being in the Nam. I guess it was something most of us guys did. Maybe to try & forget I really don't know. I felt many things for George because I knew what he might be up against. As I said things I guess were locked inside of me.

When I left your home & said my goodbyes your father pulled me aside & asked me, how is it over there? He asked me a few other things about the Nam but I really can't remember. All I said "Mr. Farawell it isn't that bad don't worry". When I learned of George's death all I could think about was what I said. I just kept it all inside. It was a very sad day for all that loved & knew him.

We hung at the lanes & played baseball in high school together. When we had practice inside the gym George & I use to shoot foul shots with the basketball. He'd always beat me & he always busted me about it. I remember how his eyes use to puff up in the summer. I use to laugh & bust him about it. I have passed the monument at times & just think what a shame that he had to leave us so young.

But he was strong enough to fulfill his duty when called upon. The boys who gave their lives were the real hero's. George was right in the letter he wrote home "when he dies in about 90 years he'll go to heaven because he already spent his time in hell, **Vietnam"**.

Thank you for the opportunity Patti to reflect.
Steven Di Gangi

---

7 May 01

Patti:

The memories of those days really came rushing back to me when I read your note and George's letter. He also wrote us right before he died—a letter that my father hid from my brother and I since it too came after he died. You probably don't know, but my brother's birthday is March 18, so, of course, I always think of him on that day as I do on many occasions throughout the years. I wish that we all had gotten the chance to see George with a wife and family. I know that he would have been a terrific father and husband. He tried to be tough on the outside, but he really was a complete mush on the inside. I certainly am a better person for knowing him and I am very happy that you still include me in your life.

I have chills all over my body and can't keep the tears from rolling down my cheeks. Good luck with the book; I probably still have the letters from George. I know that I never got rid of them; I just have to find them. If you want I will take a look.

I contacted Ronnie Kisylia and sent him a copy of your e-mail with George's letter. He had just been to the memorial in NJ that weekend and couldn't believe I was calling him. I hadn't spoken to him in 30 years—it was wild, but we had a nice talk. George is still in everyone's mind, not just because we lost him so young, but also because he touched all of our lives so deeply. I still have all the pictures from New Year's Eve that year. Do you remember that we went out that night right before he left?

Say hi to your Mom for me. Talk to you soon and if you need or want anything from me, please don't hesitate.

Love,
Barbara

PS I am going to Washington the first weekend in June and will try to go to the memorial. It was very hard for me when I went the last time we were there. I thought it would be easy, but it is extremely moving to be there as I am sure you know. Take care!!

---

7 May 2001

Patti,

Thank you for sharing that with me, I remember as if it were yesterday. I can still see the official U.S. Army car ridding past our Bergen Ave home as I was getting in my car to go to the night shift at General Motors some thirty years ago. I just knew something was wrong and when work let out at 2 am I returned home to find a note left on the kitchen table by my parents confirming my worst nightmare.

I enjoyed Rich's letter, makes me realize just how close we all were to George. I always think of the times and there were many, like George's love affair with riding buses, I don't know why he would say but I just love riding the BUS anywhere— at that time it was mostly to Elizabeth, NJ. Or the time My Grandfather passed away he lived with us at Bergen Ave so George got to know him well. His funeral was on a school day at ST. E's church at 9:00 am. As we exited the Church there was George in the last pew. That's the way he was.

Eddie Malinowsky

May 21, 2001

Patti:

Oh how I remember that day! You called me to tell me you were pregnant and you were thrilled and I for you. I remember hanging up the phone and George Chase calling to say Jimmy Crystal said the Army just came in to see your Dad. I was overwhelmed with sadness.

I also remember you saying the day you went to see George off, as the long column of soldiers filed onto the plane the only one to turn and wave was George. You said you knew he was saying good-bye.

It seems like yesterday we were all in 4th Ward Park playing paddle tennis, where has time gone? Thank you for sharing this with me.

What kind of book are you writing? What is the format? Of course, you can use my reply. I really do remember that day standing in my kitchen. It is absolutely amazing how we can go from pure happiness to the depths of disappear. George was a good kid, just a kid when he died. To this day, I am unable to watch movies about the Vietnam war. It is too real, too close.

I do not believe we "die" in the true sense. I believe we are energy and move to another time. I do feel we will see each other, not in the physical sense, but a real sense nonetheless. George is at peace. It is the sadness of not being able to share your life with him that hurts, to have watched him fulfill his dreams and grow in life. Who knows Pat, he probably is better off than we are dealing with life down here!

Keep me posted and don't be so hard on yourself.

Take care,
Diane Stancensky Pribush

August 19, 2001

Patti,

It was strange to be back in the company of old friends. There is not a day that goes by that I don't think of Georgie. What if!

I was home from the service in 66' got married in 68 Then in 69' your good friend is gone. After that, it seemed that times in Linden started to drift away. That included friends from that time. Sure once in awhile I would run into Gag, but it was different.

You cannot imagine how glad I was to see you and your family. Patti I always thought George was older than you. The same age as Gag. You and Gag are the same age. George was 2 or 3 years younger? Write soon.

Sam Iacobone

June 2, 2001

Patti,

I surely remember George, yourself and your family. I was able to attend his funeral and have visited the Vietnam Memorial on three occasions to visit George.

I would have to say my earliest memories relate to George and myself playing baseball together at Warinaco Park in Elizabeth. One year we played with the Yankees and we were co-MVP of the league. I still have a team picture that I would gladly send to you if you can give me an address. I can also remember going to your house after school and playing basketball at the corner park.

You are correct about Sr. Augustine loving us and getting us to do things for the class plays that we never thought we would do. We danced, sang, gave speeches and I am sure made fools of ourselves.

I still think about George from time to time and am very happy that you contacted me. I will try to jog my memory and contact you if I remember anything else. My wife and I now live in Clinton, N.J., which is not that far from the Poconos, after spending twenty years in Dallas, Texas. We have three children who are still in Dallas, but no grandchildren.

Please keep in touch.
Robin Kornmeyer

June 15, 2001

Hi Patti,

Yes, that classmates web site is great for looking up old schoolmates.

I am now living in Florida. I work in the Tampa area. My mother is also down here, living in New Port Richey. I am single and have no children.

My memories of George are from our years at St Elizabeth's grammar school. We were in the same class and were altar boys together. I remember him for his athletic ability. He was the person who was always picked first when choosing sides for teams. I can still recall us playing touch football on Bergen St after school.

About seven years ago, I was in Washington D.C. on business. While there, I visited the wall. I purposely looked up George's name in the index and stood in front of the engraving. I hope it gives you and your family comfort that someone would remember to do that after all these years. I also looked up Maurice O'Callahan, another St Elizabeth's classmate killed in Vietnam.

Like you, unexpectedly loosing a sibling at a young age, I can understand and appreciate you keeping that person in your thoughts. I often wonder what my brother would be like now.

You caught me on a day off. I am on my way out to catch a flight to Ft Lauderdale to visit some friends for the weekend.

Good luck with your book. Upon completion, I would like to read it. I will show my mother your note.

Give my regards to your mom.

Paul Schlicker

July 21, 2001

Patti

I remember a giant smile always on his face. His gleaming white teeth would show. An animated personality and friendly person. He was a better than average athlete. I was sadden to hear of his death, a tragic waste of a loving person.

Sincerely,

Doug Jolly

September 4, 2001

Dear Patti,

I have been trying to think of something to write and that was my problem. Don't think just write. I want to thank you for getting us all together. I received some closure on the loss of George but I will never forget him. I saw not just friends of old but a family of yours that treasured George before and after his loss. I was always appreciative of life but seeing you and your family has taken it to another level. I will thank you for that always. Good luck with your book.

Best wishes,

Friends Always,

Michael Favor Jr.

March 2, 2001

Patti,

I am sorry this reply took so long but I was not able to "SEND" mail for some time. Yes, I was at that New Years Eve Party. I found some pictures in my basement and three of them include George. If you would like them, I would be happy to have them reproduced and mail them to you.

I was living in California when Christine Hoptay, my date for the New Years Eve Party called me, and told me George was dead. I think that was the day the Vietnam War actually became REAL to me and, not just a news STORY. It was a sad day for Linden, NJ.

Mike Brown

WELCOME HOME THE RETURN

The 199th Light Infantry Brigade returned from distinguished service in Vietnam and Cambodia against a determined and aggressive enemy, and was inactivated in a ceremony October 15, 1970 on York Field at Fort Benning. The Redcatchers hence etched their name in eleven hard-won campaigns with over **750 Killed In Action** in the last sustained Infantry combat of the twentieth century.

Brigade units earned the Presidential Unit Citation, Valorous Unit Award, Meritorious Unit Commendation, two awards of the Republic of Vietnam Cross of Gallantry with Palm, and the Republic of Vietnam Civil Action Honor Medal First Class.

Taken from the Redcatcher Banquet Program Sunday May 27th 2001.

MY REFLECTIONS

As we baby boomers are passing 50 and are thinking about retirement, we need to reflect on our life and times. What we have lived through and experienced has been unreal. Could we ever imagine man landing on the moon in our lifetime? When we think back to our childhood the first thing that comes to mind is playing with our friends by our house with some kind of ball. Life was so simple.

Did we exhaust ourselves trying to give our kids everything we did not have? Is that why we need to retire early and slow down? We never seem to be satisfied. Family should be the most important thing in our lives. When we lose one member it changes us forever. No one knows what is around the corner. September 11th was a wake up call for all Americans and also a history lesson in the circle of life. Does anything seem more important then our family? We are facing war again but that is our price for freedom. Families will have to lose loved ones as we fight terrorism.

Did our soldiers die in vain? I think not. All that has happened in the past 60 years with our veterans, the fall of communism, the Berlin wall coming down, etc. I could go on and on. It all comes down to freedom.

Reality TV is so popular now. How about taking 19 year olds, dropping them in a foreign land, give them supplies to carry on their backs, put booby traps, land mines, snakes, leeches, the enemy, in their way and see who survives. Sounds like the army to me. Our veterans are the real survivors, bless them one and all.

We are FREE, and The Greatest Country in the World. United We Stand!

Thank you Veterans!!

March 2, 2016

Dear George,

I hope this book makes you proud. Your family and friends never forgot you or your kind and loving ways. You touched all of us with your spirit that is still with us today.
Till we meet again I love you.

Good night and sweet dreams...
Your loving sister,
Patti

PART 2

George T. Farawell at 19

In early October 2001, I mailed my book to a publisher and received a wonderful review back from them. It reads as follows:

Dear Ms. Enyedy,

I am pleased to report that, subject to working out the necessary agreements, A Redcatcher's Letters from Nam has been accepted for publication by one of our editors.

The review follows herein:

George Thomas Farawell was just an average nineteen-year-old boy from a middle class New Jersey family when he was drafted into the army and shipped to Vietnam. He had only served eight weeks of his tour of duty when he fell victim to a land mine. In this touching chronicle of his tragically brief life, Patricia Farawell Enyedy pays tribute to her brother, sharing the letters that he wrote as a young man away from home for the first time, bravely facing a hell no one should have to endure. Ms. Enyedy does a good job of providing interesting background information on the 199th Infantry Brigade, gives a poignant glimpse into how George's loss affected the entire family, and includes reminiscences from peers as they remember a friend over three decades of time and pay homage to a comrade-in-arms.

But the heart of this touching book lies in the innocent candor of George's own letters in which he discusses saving money, naming a mongrel dog and honestly expresses the bewilderment, anxiety and fear experienced by a normal American kid suddenly plunged into a nightmare predicament.

As a portrait of George emerges from these pages, we realize he is the boy next door, the sweetheart that will never come home, the brother and son that can never be replaced. Ms. Enyedy does her brother credit in this poignant and brave profile of a soldier.

October 20, 2001

FYI: A "redcatcher" is a soldier in the 199th Infantry Brigade.

Mon, 18 Mar 2002

From the publication of my book about a wonderful young man, I have reunited with many old friends. They have supported me by finding each other and writing heartwarming reflections of their friend. Emotions buried for years surface again and we are young. Facing life's challenges with our "we know it all attitude, we are cool" voices of the 1960's. We lost many friends to the war and most of George's friends were in the military too. I am glad to say most returned to live wonderful productive lives and live for their friend. I am proud of each of them. I know coming to with their feelings again in middle age was worth it to have all of us realize, any day now could be the end. Live life to the fullest and everyday remember some one less fortunate.

I have been adopted by the 199th Light Infantry Brigade as a sister to all, these remarkable men who have had to live with so many horrible memories went on to live their lives to the fullest. Some good days and many bad days but moving on always. Tomorrow will be better. They still give each other moral support and are still finding their brothers today! We recently found Jose in Florida. He is dying of cancer but the brothers got him involved looking up pictures. In a few weeks there is a spark in his emails. I know one of these days I will see my brother in one of their pictures.

Memorial Day 2002, I was invited to attend their memorial at the Wall in Washington, DC. Each year, The Redcatcher's gather to remember their fallen comrades, to place their combat patch for each vet and read off the names of the KIA's. I read George's name. It was so emotional, I told them of my book and it was dedicated to them, all of them for never forgetting their brothers.

That evening we attended their dinner buffet and I had a book signing. One by one the Redcatchers came over with tears in their eyes to get a copy of my book and say hello to me and my brother Stephen. I was also awarded a writing award for excellence **Redcatchers Writing Award that evening.**

I wish I could reach more families like myself to let them know all that still goes on in their loved one's memory with websites, books, magazine articles, etc. The Redcatchers have kept me in the loop with all of their correspondence and I have found many who were with my brother remembering the puppy he had but not really remembering his face. The veterans who lived the whole year kept each other alive. It is harder to remember the ones who only lived with them for 8 weeks and were going home. One veteran wrote me after reading my book after Memorial Day last year, that they could have been his letters. "All they all wanted to do was go home, and George was one of the one **"to go home early."**

I also am still hearing from childhood and high school friends some I don't remember but they are compelled to write and I love it. I read every letter to my mother who has macular degeneration now and has no central vision. She lives with me and my husband in NC and I am so glad I can take care of her. She is amazed how many remember her boy and I am finally at peace with his passing. I answered his call to do something with my time and get involved.

In Book 2, I have found more Redcatchers who were with him and possibly know who Glenn is. By reading the following email from Redcatchers, family and friends you will again join my journey.

REFLECTIONS OF FAMILY
AND FRIENDS

After my Book was published

The following are Reflections to Remember, which came after the book was published.

March 18, 2002

Hello, Patti.

You probably don't remember me. I was one of the younger kids in the Linden neighborhood where you grew up.

My name is Billy Margel and I grew up at 801 Essex Ave., on the corner across the street from John Ostertiki and across the street from Pete Kardash and next door to Freddie Haviland. I don't know if you know any of those names but they were all a bit older than me so maybe you do.

I remember playing at the park, now named in honor of your brother George. Your brother Steve was closer to my age (a few years older) but he was around and we played basketball and touch football and whiffle ball. I remember one summer day Steve brought me over to your home and we had a peanut butter and jelly sandwich together. I really thought that was cool because Steve was older and therefore cool. (I even remember your dog, Taffy.) I also remember your Dad bought my father's car once. A white and gold Chevy Impala I think it was.

I remember George coming over to the park every once in a while, too. We usually cleared out then because the bigger kids usually started playing then and we simply weren't big enough to compete.

I do remember George quite vividly, though, with his short blond hair and all. He never bothered us younger kids much so he wasn't a bully or anything. He seemed like a nice guy. I remember his best friend was Richie Gagliardi ("Gags") who lived over by 4th Ward Park. I guess by the time I was old enough to hang out at the park George had pretty much outgrown it but he did come down once in a while.

I remember the day I found out George died in Vietnam. My friend was a paperboy and he told me he saw it in the Daily Journal. We went over to the park that evening, I guess I was 14 at the time, and talked to my friends about it. We were all pretty sad. I remember going to George's funeral mass with my friend Joe Petrovich at St. Elizabeth's.

I live in Clark now but I go by the old neighborhood once in a while. It's nice that Linden renamed the park for him. Now no one will forget the sacrifice he made.

I was on the web, reading about the IA Drang battle in Vietnam, and started wondering about George. So, I looked it up and found your name on Redcatcher.com. I noticed that today is the 33rd anniversary of George's death. It's hard to believe that much time has passed. Every once in a while I think about George and how sad it is that he died so young. I am sure he is at peace. I have a lot of respect for him and what he did. I will never forget him.

I hope you are doing well with your book of George's letters. I hope you have found his friends that were with him in Vietnam and they are able to help you out. Say hello to Steve for me. I hope you are all doing well.

Bill Margel
Neighbor

March 21, 2002

Hello, Patti.

I read your book about your brother George, **"A Redcatcher's Letters from Nam"**.

I think it is a touching and appropriate testimony and tribute to his life. I am sure he would be quite proud of it. You have done a wonderful job.

There are really a lot of great things in the book but the highlight for me is the letters George sent to you and your family while he was in Viet Nam. They truly bring his experience there to life. They portray a young man caught up in something he probably does not want to be part of and something he probably doesn't fully understand. I admire him for doing his duty nonetheless. I can see the progression into more and more dangerous situations from those letters, until his last few speak about the land mine dangers that would eventually take his life.

It was great to read how much he appreciated all the things your family and others sent to him. I am sure it was a great comfort to him to know you were all so supportive and concerned about his well-being. One can see a little bit of cockiness in those letters (what else would you expect from a 20 year old raised in Linden?) but there is also a lot of respect and a renewed appreciation for the life he had in Linden. That, in itself, is a testimony to the way he was raised. Your parents must be immensely proud of that.

I knew before I started it was not going to be an easy read. Much like you as you were researching materials, I also experienced a wide range of emotions while reading it. There were tears in my eyes at times but there were also passages that brought a smile. When George writes that he is going to look like Buckwheat was one instance among others where I had to chuckle. And the way he sometimes signed his letters, The Main Man, Your Fighting Son made me smile, too. But there was always the "Love, George" and the many "Miss You All" to close his letters.

By reading these letters, I get a close and personal look at George that I never had when I knew him in Linden. His remarks about Steve going to school and Steve's behavior show a big brother concerned about the welfare of his younger sibling. Just the fact that he wrote so often, to you, to your Mom & Dad, to Steve, to your husband, provides a glimpse of the type of person he was: an individual who cared.

Thank you for sharing these with the world. I know they are personal and it must have taken a lot of courage to put them in a book for all to see. But it is a good thing to do. Now all will know what kind of person we lost.

A flood of memories came to me as I read. The pictures you have included are stories unto themselves. I liked the picture of you, George and Steve in front of your home on Easter Sunday. It reflects the innocence you mention that we all had growing up in that neighborhood. The picture you included of you and George just before he left reminds me of how pretty you were. (I think all the boys in the neighborhood were aware of how pretty you were. I think it had a lot to do with your blond hair.) The picture of your parents at the park dedication reminded me of my being there and what a solemn ceremony it was. I was actually standing over by the Malinowsky house on that day. And the pictures of George remind me of the person I knew.

The present day pictures also are great. Steve looks the same (except for some gray) and Richie Gagliardi's and Eddie Malinowsky's hair are both all white. I guess we all get old but these folks will remain forever young in my memories. That is how I knew them.

I remember the stereo you mention that George bought for your parents. When I was in your home that summer day when Steve invited me in for a peanut butter and jelly sandwich, I remember him actually turning it on. I think he put on WABC or something and we listened to some music while we ate. I think he was showing it off.

Every time you mention the park it reminds of the great childhood years I spent there with all the neighborhood kids. We had a lot of fun there. A lot of it was due to the fact that it was so stable. All the kids were around year after year. That is a tribute to the mothers and fathers that raised us. Sure, we got into some mischief but it was nothing too serious. It was a great place to grow up in.

There were a lot of things included in the book I did not know. I didn't know that Richie Gagliardi led the way to have the park dedicated to George. It was a great thing to do and I wish I could have been there for the re-dedication in 1999. I think you are right when you say there were angels in your house. You learned of your pregnancy the day before George died. One life begins, another tragically ends. (Something similar happened to me. My son James was born a few days after my wife's father died.)

Your explanations of the history 199th, the meaning of the patch, the inclusion of the reflections of his Viet Nam comrades and the reflections of his friends and family at home all contribute to the story in an eloquent, touching and meaningful way.

I have been lucky over the years. I have not had an immediate family member taken away from me yet. My parents (both 81) are doing well in the Toms River area. My sister, Bernadette is living in the Baltimore area. I have been married for 7 1/2 years to Mary, a girl from Linden, and I have 2 beautiful children, Lauren (almost 5) and James (3).

I can't imagine the pain and grief you all went through when George died. This book has certainly shown it, though. I admire your family's courage and ability to cope with such a tragedy.

I am glad to hear that your mother is with you and that Steve is doing well. I think it's great that you have retired relatively young. It's a small world. My sister-in-law, Sue, lives in Stroudsburg, too. She lives right off Route 80 (exit 53 I think), on a one-block street called Barry Street. We get up there a couple of times a year.

The late sixties and early seventies were uncertain times in America and they touched us even in Linden. The racial tensions Steve mentions in his reflections and George's death in the war brought these troubles directly into our homes and lives. We were a nation tearing itself apart. Yet we survived. George's sacrifice was a tremendous contribution to that survival process. His death was tragic and may have been senseless in a way but it brought us closer to the ultimate conclusion of that conflict. We must struggle to understand it.

When I look at my children I realize the frailty of life. Your personal "reflections" near the end of your book encompass a lot of my feelings today. Family and freedom is very important and dear to us. We are a great and free nation and unfortunately we must fight to preserve that greatness and freedom. People who are lost in the service of this country to preserve those ideals are all heroes and your brother George Thomas Farawell is now part of those ideals and what makes them noble.

I have printed a copy of your book. I plan to bring it to my parent's house this Easter weekend. I'm sure it will bring back a lot of memories for them, too.

Someday, when my kids are a little older, I'm going to bring them over to the old neighborhood where we grew up. I'll tell those stories about us and bring them to the park. I'll show them George's memorial and explain to them what it means and how important it is. Eventually, I will have them read your book and they will get a much clearer and deeper meaning of what life in the United States is all about.

I don't really see many of the kids from the neighborhood anymore, although I wish I did. I know we could have a lot of laughs. Maybe someday I'll bump into a few of them. (As a matter of fact, I ran into Kathy Kenny a few months back in the Linden Pathmark. She is Tom Kenney's younger sister. They lived on the corner of Bergen and Lincoln streets.) If I do run into anyone, I promise I will tell them about your book. I'm sure they will be very interested. It is a worthwhile and enjoyable experience.

I know I have carried on here a bit but there were a lot of things I needed to say. Written words are a way of interpreting emotion and although they can never adequately reflect the deepest feelings, they do allow for a route of escape and relief.

Once again, thank you for writing that book and letting me know about it. It was great to hear from you. Tell your mother and Steve I said Hello. I wish you all well.

I'll close with my most vivid memory of George. It was probably mid to late spring. I remember being at the park, probably playing basketball. George came striding into the park from Bergen Street. He had on his Linden High Varsity jacket, a pair of tan work pants and high top sneakers. I remember his short blond hair and a big smile. I remember him a grabbing basketball and I can imagine him saying, "Let's play."

Sincerely,
Bill Margel
Neighbor

Patti,

I received the book on Friday and read it on Saturday. It is still very difficult to read, but I did get through it. It is amazing!

I know the Supervisor of Social Studies in Linden and just got off the Phone with her and she is going to order it for the library at Linden High School and maybe to be used in the classes. I think it would be great for the students to read a book about someone from LHS. I hope you don't mind that I called her, but I do believe it has a place in LHS. Do you agree? She seemed thrilled about it.

Patti, you really did a good thing. Everyone loves this book--it is such a tribute to you and your relationship with George. The sadness is that we all lost him, but this is the best thing that you could have done. It reminds us, as you said, that life is precious and we have to take each moment and live it to the fullest.

Barbara Pawlowski
George's girlfriend

Wed, 10 Apr 2002

Hi Patti,

I sat down last night and started reading the book. I didn't put it down till I finished it. It's a beautiful tribute to George. There are a lot of memories wrapped up in that book. Soldiers who went to Viet Nam lived in a hell of their own while over there. I know, I married one and it wasn't easy when he first came home. Still years later, I know a lot of what he saw over there still eats away at him. I too read the book thru tears and memories and sadness. I guess we all went thru a little hell, even the girlfriends and wives that were left behind, not knowing from day to day if they were alive or not, if you would get a letter from them soon, or if that dreaded military car would show up outside your house. Next time I'm in NJ, I'll stop by the park and visit "George". He truly has some remarkable friends and a family who still loves and thinks of him.

And I also noted in your book he was born on Jan. 27th.... Funny, Patti, that's my birthday to, and also the day I got married.

I'm heading back to NJ in a few weeks to visit my sister. Please stay in touch, and Chick sends his best and his love......Still looks the same. Just a little older.

Hugs
Elaine Artitus
My friend

April 15, 2002

Hello Patti,

I received the book you wrote several days ago about George. I read it the first day I got it. Thank you for writing this book. It is great! It's an honor for your Brother and to all of us that were with the 199th. Tears flowed from my eyes while reading it. My wife Nikki read it also and she cried.

Thanks again,
Wayne Garrett
(Redcatcher)

June 16 Apr 2002
Hi Patti,

I purchased your book off the Internet. It was very easy to purchase on-line and I received it in the mail in about 5 days. The book is great and I learned a lot.

Congratulations on a great book.

Rob Ciano
My Second cousin

April 16, 2002
Patti,

All I can say is "WOW." This book is really touching everyone that reads it--what a legacy! You are wonderful.

Have a great day! I would like to come to see you before you leave for SC.

Love,
Barbara Pawlowski
George's Girlfriend

April 17. 2002

PATTY

I'M SO HAPPY ALL TURNED OUT OK WITH THE BOOK & ALL. I WILL DEFINATLY GET ONE (CAN'T WAIT TO READ IT) GEORGE WOULD HAVE BEEN SO PROUD OF YOU. HE HAS A GOOD SISTER & SOMEHOW I FEEL HE'S LOOKING DOWN AT YOU WITH A SMILE ON HIS FACE.
HAVE A GREAT DAY & KEEP IN TOUCH. OK?

STEVE DIGANGI
George's friend

April 19, 2002

PATTY,

WHAT IS THE BOOK TITLE AND WHO IS TAKING ORDERS AT THIS TIME. I WOULD LOVE TO HAVE A COPY.

THANKS,
RICK JONES
D/4/12 AUG69-JAN70

April 19, 2002

Your book is a very good idea I made it back and I know many name's on the wall my heart goes out to the many families behind those names.

My wife kept all my letters and we recently read them and type them up, we may do the same thing. I've got 264 typed pages from

Vietnam alone, & we weren't married at the time. I find they're more of a journal than love letters.

Have you ever been to the 199th's reunion? You along with other fallen brothers' families are welcome. They hold a special place in our hearts as we annually remember them. The 199th is on its 34th reunion I believe. Once you been to one you can't stop coming to them. The reunion info is listed on the web site and the dates are May 24th to May 27th.

My name is Dennis Lietha from Minn. live on a farm and I was a member of D troop 17th Cav. 199th LIB. 69\70

Dennis & Rita

April 19, 2002

Hi Patty

I was class of 68 did Nam 69-70 we lost Otto Ostenfeld from our class he was a marine died 6/69.

Lane Robert Schaab

April 21, 2002

Sorry Patti, I don't remember Glenn! I need a last name and I would probably remember him. I won't be going to DC Memorial day! It's a long way to go from Oklahoma.

Take care,
Wayne Garrett
Redcatcher

April 22, 2002

Patti,
Just finished your book, I had tears in my eyes the whole time. My memories are mostly of all you guys when you were young and I baby sat for your Mom, but I can remember his smile and blond hair .You did a beautiful job, anyone who reads it, can feel the love running from those pages.

Love,
Jane Muroski
My first cousin

Monday, April 22, 2002 09:13:38 PM

Subject: Great book

Hi Patti,

Just finished Redcatcher's Letter's...You really did an excellent job on describing that awful day, and the painful days that followed.

Thanks' for being so open and candid.

Mark Donaldson
Friend

Mon, 22 Apr 2002

Mom E:

First - it was wonderful to see you yesterday at the studio! I'm glad we got to say hi at least! You look wonderful - as do your beautiful grandchildren!

I can't believe that you're book is on Amazon! I can't wait to get my copy & read it.

Looking forward to it! Congratulations! I'm so proud & happy for you!

Love,
Donna Perozzi
Friend of my son

Mon, 22 Apr 2002

Hi Pat,

That's Great! I was in Borders the other day and was hoping to see your book. I bought 1 book there on, of all things, ancient mythology. Have you tried contacting the Military Book Club? I just bought 3 new books and 3 DVDs from them. Your sales will explode, if they start listing your book. I still have not received your book that I ordered from 1st books.com. Hopefully, it will arrive this week.

John Hoffart
Friend of mine

Tribute to a Brother, April 23, 2002

Reviewer: William Margel from Clark, NJ USA

"A Redcatcher's Letters from Nam" is a heartfelt presentation of a family's loss.

George T. Farawell was a young man from New Jersey who died in Viet Nam. This book, written by his sister, is a touching blend of the past and present, enveloped by the emotional struggle of dealing with a tragic loss.

The story is simple yet powerful. A synopsis of the 199th Light Infantry Brigade is a fitting tribute to all those who served in its ranks. Snapshots of what is was like growing up in an industrial New Jersey town identifies George as a person like many of us. Reflections of family and friends exemplify the pain and sadness and loss all of George's friends and family experienced as a result of his death.

The essence of this book, however, is exactly what the title tells us. It is the almost daily letters George wrote home during his tour in Viet Nam that are the highlight. These make George come to life for all of us who read them. They are personal but are presented in their original content and by reading them we realize the type of person George was.

I highly recommend reading this book. It is a correct and fitting tribute to a young man who completed his duty as a soldier. Indeed, it is a tribute to all those who have served honorably in the ranks of our nation's armed services. It makes us realize the struggles we must endure to preserve our humanity.

The Story of a Typical Vietnam Soldier, April 22, 2002

Reviewer: Barbara Pawlowski from Rahway, NJ United States

What a sad and wonderful story! This book is a story about a typical 20-year-old soldier in Vietnam. It illustrates, through his own personal words, the conditions that these men experienced and the emotional trauma that they felt every day. It also tells of the family and how they tried to cope with having their oldest son in the midst of a war so far from home. I knew George while in high school and reading these letters from him gives me a whole new meaning and perspective on what these young men went through while they were in Vietnam. George was only there for eight weeks and these are "his" letters, but they are "everyone's." They tell a story of a typical soldier. This is a book for everyone who remembers those times and everyone who wants to learn about them. It is a truly touching book written by his sister. I recommend this book to all; it is a must read.

April 27, 2002
Hi Pat,

We received your book on Tuesday. I happened to be home that night, so I took the book into the sunroom to read. I just finished reading the back cover when Ginny walked in and said, "I was going to read it". So of course I relinquished the book to her. She read it all the way through the letters, and then finished it last night. She often commented to me on different parts of the book. I then started reading. You wrote a beautiful book. The hardest part for me was reading the "Saying Good Bye" chapter. I could not continue and put the book down to gain my composure. I could not bring myself to continue with the letters and it was getting late, so I will try again, maybe tonight.

John Hoffart
Friend of mine

May 2, 2002

WOWWWWWWWWW.
I JUST FINISHED YOUR BOOK & IT WAS VERY TOUCHING. GEORGE WOULD BE PROUD OF YOU AS I CAN SAY I AM. IT TOOK ME A FEW DAYS TO FINISH IT. THERE WERE TIMES I HAD TO PUT IT DOWN. I WANTED TO TAKE IT TO WORK & READ IT. BUT I KNEW I JUST COULDN'T THERE WERE TOO MANY TEARS. GEORGE WILL ALWAYS BE IN MY HEART & THOUGHTS FOR WHAT HE DONE WAS SOMETHING OF HONOR. HE WENT & DID WHAT HE HAD TO DO EVEN IF HE THOUGHT IT WAS A WASTE OF TIME. I CAN IDENTIFY IN THE MANY THINGS GEORGE WENT THROUGH DURING HIS

SHORT TIME IN THE NAM. HE WAS SCARED AS WE ALL WERE BUT HE WAS A MAN & JUST DID WHAT HE HAD TO DO. IN THE NAM 99% OF WHAT GETS U THROUGH IS ALL LUCK. I WAS GLAD THAT HE SOUNDED STRONG IN HIS LETTERS & THAT HE ALWAYS KEPT THE FAMILY VALUES DURING ALL HE HAD GONE THROUGH. HE'S MY HERO AS HE IS FOR SO MANY OTHERS WHAT HE LEARNED IN HIS SHORT TIME THERE MOST PEOPLE WILL NEVER LEARN. I AM ALSO SO GLAD & PROUD OF WHAT YOU DONE WITH THE WRITING OF THIS BOOK. I'D LIKE TO THANK YOU FOR THAT. IF YOU HAD WRITTEN THIS BOOK 30 YRS AGO THERES NO WAY I COULD HAVE READ IT BUT TIME REPAIRS WOUNDS SOMEWHAT & LIFE HAS TO GO ON. I HAD TOLD MANY OF MY FRIENDS ABOUT THE BOOK & THEY CAN'T WAIT
TO READ IT. WELL PATTY I HOPE WE CAN KEEP IN TOUCH AND THANK YOU SO VERY MUCH FOR WHAT YOU HAVE DONE. WHAT A TRIBUTE TO A GREAT PERSON GEORGE FARAWELL YOUR BROTHER.

STEVEN DI GANGI
Vietnam Vet
Friend of George

May 2, 2002

Today I received a phone call from 1stbooks with a response to Press Release of my book. Ken Boswell from Heads up America Radio wants to do an interview with me on 5/23 the day before we leave for DC. I am nervous; it is live with call ins. He is going to read my book and get back to me.

I did it a live show and I had 3 Redcatchers call in.

May 22, 2002

Good Luck tomorrow with the show. I finished the book on Sunday (couple of hours to read it all) I liked it a lot. I only remember George vaguely. I was 7 going on 8 when he went into the service. I remember him in his uniform and remember how young he was. You did a fantastic job on the book and provided a lot of insight. Bob is almost done reading it and Chris is waiting to read it. All of his kids want to read it. I think that they will learn from this.

Chris has told me he has already bragged in school about having a famous "Aunt" who is an author. A couple of his friends have expressed interest in reading the book as well.

Diane Bechtle
My cousin

Mon, 3 Jun 2002

Hi Patti:

I was wondering how you made out in Washington, D.C.? Also.....

I read your book and so did Richard. What an astounding book it is. I had a lump in my throat the whole time. I even read through the letters again. I was so flattered that you thought enough of the both of us to put us in. Your mention of Richard, myself and Natalie were awesome.

Congratulations on your best seller.

Love,

Jenn Gagliradi
My friend

Patti

    I read your book and loved it. Here is a letter I wrote that may amaze you. I hope I knew what I was talking about!

Sat, 25 May 2002

Dear Patti,

Hi! I sat down and read your book last night.... it is a wonderful Tribute to George. Walt served in Vietnam a couple of years after George and never talked about it until Platoon and the other movies about Nam came out. Reading George's letters was like hearing Walt describe what it was like over there. I wish Walt's family had saved some of his letters.

In Walt's things, I have some of the pictures he took while over in Nam... and I found an envelope with stationery from Nam where Walt had written some of his thoughts, but must have never sent them to anyone. There is also a couple page letters with a few notes from others guys who were serving with him. It's sad to think of what they went through....

Well, I just wanted to let you know I enjoyed the book. Hope to talk with you soon.

Love,
Donna Calkins
Cousin

Hi Aunt Patti --

    How are u? I've been meaning to e-mail you anyway, but things have been so hectic with sports and the end of the year and finals and everything. I hope all is well with you, Grandma Mary, and everyone else.

I read the book that you wrote the first night dad gave it to me, and it was really good. I learned a lot about my uncle and his experiences in the war, and tears were rolling down my cheeks the whole time I was reading it. It's kind of like when we learn things in history class, no one ever realizes that these were real people that went through all of these experiences and wars, and these people had families that loved them and feared for them. They just always seem like big events that happened in the past. And I had never really thought about what it must have been like for you to deal with having your brother away at war, not knowing from each day to the next what could possibly be going on. I kept relating what you said in the book to how I would have felt if that was my brother that was over there, and I can't even begin to imagine how hard that would have been. Thank you for sharing all of that with me through your book.

I'm really glad I had the opportunity to read all of it.

Love,
Ali Farawell
My niece

Fri, 31 May 2002

MEMORIAL DAY 2002

HELLO PATRICIA,

I JUST WANTED YOU TO KNOW I JUST FINISHED YOUR BOOK. I WAITED TIL I WAS OFF WORK UNTIL I READ IT. I COULDN'T PUT IT DOWN TILL I FINISHED IT. WHAT A GREAT MEMORIAL YOUR BROTHER WOULD BE PROUD. I WAS VERY GLAD WE MET I JUST WISH WE HAD MORE TIME TO TALK. I MISS AND LOVE MY OLDEST BROTHER SO MUCH AND I ALSO WANT TO FIND ANYONE THAT WAS WITH HIM THE DAY HE WAS KIA, I WANT TO KNOW DID HE SUFFER OR DID HE DIE INSTANTLY. I WAS 15 YEARS OLD

WHEN HE DIED AND I NEVER UNDERSTOOD THIS WAR AND WHY MY BROTHER HAD TO DIE. MY PARENTS NEVER GOT TO SEE THE WALL IN WASHINGTON AND I ALMOST DIED TWICE LAST YEAR AND WHEN I WAS IN THE HOSPITAL ALL I COULD THINK OF WAS THAT I NEEDED TO GO TO WASHINGTON TO SEE THE WALL. SO LAST YEAR I GOT IN MY CAR AND WENT THERE BY MYSELF, IT WAS SOMETHING I HAD TO DO, I WAS SCARED SINCE I NEVER WENT BY MYSELF ANYWHERE BUT I MET SOME WONDERFUL VETS THAT WALKED, HELPED ME FIND MY BROTHERS NAME AND HELD ME AND COMFORTED ME.

WHAT A BEAUTIFUL MEMORIAL BUT LIKE YOU I WANT PEOPLE TO KNOW AND REMEMBER WHO JOSE ANTONIO CARRION WAS NOT JUST A NAME ON THE WALL. HE RISKED HIS LIFE TO SAVE HIS STAFF SEARGANT (NEW YORKER) AND LOST HIS LIFE. HE WAS THE BEST BROTHER ANYONE WOULD WANT ALWAY'S THINKING OF OTHERS. I HAVE FIVE OTHER BROTHERS AND 3 OF THEM HAVE YET TO SEE THE WALL, MY WISH IS TO GO TO THE WALL WITH ALL OF THEM NEXT MEMORIAL DAY.

WELL I MUST GO TO MANY THINGS TO DO TODAY ON MY DAY OFF. SAY HI TO YOUR FAMILY AND TO YOUR BROTHER STEPHEN WHO I PLAN ON WRITING TO SOON. TAKE CARE AND THANK YOU AGAIN FOR A WONDERFUL BOOK.

GOD BLESS
YOLANDA CARRION BUSTAMANTE
(Gold Star Redcatcher Sister)

June 2002

Hello Everyone:

To try and put into words the trip to DC, it was awesome..... more gratifying than I ever imagined. I just wish my mom could have been there.

Thursday, I did a live talk radio show from NC with Ken Bagwell of Heads up America. I was nervous at first but he put me at ease immediately and it went great.........
He used my book as a lead in for the Memorial Day Weekend. I had 3 Redcatcher's call in and comment.

Sunday AM we went to the Vietnam Memorial Wall and cards were placed on each of the 750 KIA from the 199th LIB. We then went to a grassy knoll where veterans read all the names. I was asked to read George's name and say something if I wanted. I read the dedication from my book and told them a year ago; I did not know what a redcatcher was and now I have all this extended family.

YOLANDA CARRION BUSTAMANTE another sister was there also, she spoke and we both carried the wreath to the center of the monument for the dedication.

I had a book signing that night at the dinner and one by one they came to buy a book and thank me............ for what I have done for the Redcatcher's..............
They each hugged me and cried, all of them. I met the Lt. who put George on the chopper and his Sgt. at the time. I met a farmer from MN who wants to write a book and wants me to help, we met Ram from TX who was the medic, Poncho from CA who has a website and George is on it, a vet from the next town over from where Ell was born in NY state, we met families of the vets, who all were so pleased that we were there.

There were so many attendees at the last minute they had to add another room. After dinner, a gentleman came to get me and escorted me into the other room. I was introduced as I walked in and was called to the podium. I was presented a plaque with the inscription **"Patricia Enyedy Redcatcher's Award for Writing Excellence"** I was stunned and the tears flowed..........

Walking back into the other room I got a round of applause for all the vets knew I was getting the award.

Also given the award was Bob Fromme who helped me so much in finding people and guiding me. We had a wonderful talk and I made so many new friends. I hope to be instrumental in telling other gold member families how wonderful these vets are in remembering their lost loved ones. They want to touch all of the families and let them know they never forgot.............

I have heard from many of them already, here is one...

Email is from: RICKY W. JONES
May 1, 2002

Book Title: A REDCATCHER'S LETTERS FROM NAM
Message:

PATTI, I RECEIVED THE BOOK THIS AFTERNOON ON FED-UPS, OR WHATEVER, AND COULDN'T PUT IT DOWN TILL I FINISHED IT. THOSE EIGHT WEEKS WERE A LIFETIME TO GEORGE EVEN THOUGH HE KEPT THEM CALM AND COLLECTED IN HIS LETTERS. HE WAS JUST AS ALL OF US GRUNTS WERE IN DELTA COMPANY; ALWAYS GLAD TO SEE THE SUNRISE THE NEXT DAY. GEORGE, BY ALL THAT I KNOW AND BELIEVE, WAS A VERY HONORABLE "BOY" THAT WAS CAUGHT UP INTO THE TRAP THAT SO MANY HAD TO TRY TO ENDURE DURING THAT TERRIBLE WAR. I ADMIT THAT I CRIED ALL THE WAY THRU THE BOOK AND WILL AGAIN WHEN I REREAD IT. I'M SURE I WILL READ IT COUNTLESS TIMES BECAUSE I HAD ALL OF THOSE FEELINGS THAT GEORGE EXPRESSED IN HIS LETTERS AND THOSE I KNEW HE WAS FEELING WITHOUT PUTTING THEM INTO WORDS. HE WAS ALWAYS SCARED AS WE ALL WERE. FEAR KEPT US ALIVE AS LONG AS FATE AND LUCK RAN WITH US AS INDIVIDUALS. WE ALL HAD A NUMBER AND GEORGE'S WAS CALLED THAT DAY IN MARCH 1969. THANKS TO MEN LIKE HIM THE UNIT GAINED MORE INTELLIGENCE, CUNNING AND A BIGGER REASON FOR "PAYBACK" TO MAKE UP, IN OUR MINDS, A REASON TO CARRY ON. THANK YOU SO MUCH FOR SHARING GEORGE'S LETTERS WITH ALL BECAUSE THEY MEAN EVERYTHING TO A VIETNAM VETERAN THAT GOT EVEN CLOSE TO COMBAT.
MY LOVE TO YOU AND ALL YOUR FAMILY,
RICKY W. JONES,
D/4/12/199TH AUG69-JAN70

June 2002

Hi Friends:

How can I ever say thank you for all you have done for me. You have all given me a piece of yourself that I will treasure always. I feel this connection that is so heartwarming. I have a new appreciation of the American Veteran. I have always been patriotic but now even more so.

Poncho, I have gone back to your website and now when I look at those pictures of those young soldiers I have a new appreciation for all of you. To see your young innocent faces, (like George, if I would have gotten his pictures back) is great.

My award will be hung with pride in my home. I was so surprised. Thank you so very much.

Some of you have already sent me emails after you read my book. I hope each of you do so for my journal.

I would like to donate my book to the Redcatcher's Museum, is there one in Ft. Benning?

I know you have all the names of the KIA's but do you have addresses for all the families? Do they know the wonderful work that you do to remember their loved ones? If any of you have an idea of me being active in some way for the Redcatcher's let me know. I will be there next year.

Let me tell you a few funny stores: I was asked by 2 vets at the dinner who are going to Vietnam to join them! I have to tell you all, I am an American Princess. No sweating, bugs, snakes, dirt, etc. for me. I will pass on Nam and move to NC in a few months.

One table had vets who were tattooed with the patch that day and wanted to take me the next day for mine. I passed. How great was that!

I am reading UP COUNTRY right now about Nam. I don't know how realistic it is but it is giving me insight at how is it today and back then. I don't think I could have read it before.

Yolanda the sister of Jose Carrion, and I became fast friends. She and I have already emailed each other.

I would love to receive the newsletter and become a member. Send me info please.

I have been asked to speak at the NJ Vietnam Memorial in the fall and my book will be in the Education Museum. Their website is beautiful, check it out. Njvm.com.

Well thank you again for your friendship and the kindness you showed to my family.

Love, Patti

PS My new email is penyedy@yahoo.com

Re: Thank you........
Date: Thu, 6 Jun 2002
From: "Clay Crowder"

Hi Patti
    There are two places where we have things. One is at Ft Benning and the other is at Camp Shelby, Mississippi. We are a wonderful family we live had fun and died together and anyone who has a loved one who was killed in action will be accepted just like you were there.

I did not get to make the reunion this year I have just retired from my job at Fort Rucker, Al after almost 23 years there. I retired from the army in January 1977 now 25 years it does not seem that long. I was one of the old man with the 199th I was 30 years old when I arrived at Redcatcher. There are family groups on the internet but out of my head I cannot remember. Go to google.com and search KIA Vietnam it may be a few down the line.

Check out Redcatcher.org on the front page there is info on membership and newsletter comes out 2 times each year.

Take care and God Bless
Clay Crowder

Clay passed away since my book was published. He was the start of my writing and my first contact with the Redcatchers in 2001.

June 5, 2002

Hi Patty,

It makes my heart so happy to hear from you. You are inspiring to all veterans. I really enjoyed meeting you and your family at the reunion. My hands trembled my heart cried and my brow perspired when I finished reading your book.

I felt like you had written about my letters to my wife and my mother. I guess we all had simple lives and loving families we wanted to come home to. Some of our comrades went to our real home to guide the rest of us. Our friends at our parish cried when I read some passages in the book.

Patti & Ell we love you and are your friends forever.
Regards to all your family,
Pancho & Irene Ramirez
(Redcatcher)

Date: Thu, 6 Jun 2002

Hi Patti,

I read your book and think it is great...Good Job!!!...My daughter, Amy took it to school recently, because they were learning about the Vietnam War.

Barbara Saccente
Cousin

Date: Thu, 6 Jun 2002

Hello, Patti,

I'm glad to hear your trip to DC went well. I'm sure it was an emotional and enjoyable experience. It's good that you got to meet some of George's comrades.

Well, NC is a nice place to retire to. Are you near the ocean? The only worry there is hurricanes. Otherwise it is very nice. I've been to the Outer Banks a couple of times for vacation and enjoyed it immensely.

Good luck. Take care. Say hello to Steve for me.

Bill Margel
Friend

Sent: Sunday, June 9, 2002

Subject: Your brother George.

Hi Patti,

I read your message about George and wanted to let you know about my memories. George and I both had Mr. Richardson for Printing class back in High School and though he was a couple of grades behind me we got along good mainly because we both had a mutual pal (Ray Place) who we joked with. I'm not too sure what happened to Ray, I do know that when I was in Japan I visited him after he got wounded in Nam at Camp Zama. He was sedated and never knew I came to visit him.

I was not aware of George's death until I got back from overseas. My brother Ronnie came to me and told me that he was angry with himself because he and George had started pushing each other after some basketball game and he felt bad about the way they had last seen each other. My brother was in Thailand when he heard about George's death. His regret remains with him to this day. In my case, I went to Washington DC in 1992 to place a baseball below the name of Ed West who went to Soehl Jr High and someone I played catch with. I also brought with me some printing letter types that spelled out "FRIEND" and placed it in a small pillbox below George's name. I sometimes go to the Wall website and look at his name and all the other men and women who gave of themselves.

I hope knowing this helps you in some way and I hope your life is full of fond and loving memories of George.

Take care of yourself,
Rob Guerra
My friend

Subject: Re: Brothers
Date: Wed, 19 Jun 2002

Dear Patti:
I will be there. I just got my book today and I can't put it down. Well done, my dear friend. You did an excellent job. If I could do l/4 of what you have done, I would be happy.

Please stop in my website. I will send you another invite and password. I have 18 pages of pictures so far, and you are there too from our reunion.

Till then,
Angela Colletti
My classmate she passed away

June 20, 2002

PATTY,

   I WAS HONORED TO HAVE RECIEVED THIS EMAIL. IT MAKES ME FEEL GOOD THAT YOU HAVE ME IN YOUR MAILING LIST. IN CASE I HAVEN'T ALREADY TOLD YOU, I WAS REALLY REALLY HONORED TO HAVE BEEN ACKNOWLEDGED IN YOUR BOOK AND YOU USING MY LETTER TO YOU LAST YEAR. BOB FROMME WAS HERE EARLIER THIS YEAR FOR A SHORT VISIT. WE HAD A GOOD TIME THAT DAY. I WAS GLAD HE WAS IN THE BOOK, TOO.
   PANCHO SENT ME PHOTOS FROM THE MEMORIAL DAY REUNION AND I WAS PLEASED TO SEE YOU IN SOME OF THEM. I SURE WISH I HAD BEEN THERE TO MEET YOU BUT TIME AND MONEY DID NOT ALLOW US TO MAKE THE TRIP THIS YEAR. YOU WERE IN THE COMPANY OF SOME VERY FINE PEOPLE THERE AND I'LL BET THEY WERE ALL GLAD YOU CAME.

I HOPE TO HEAR FROM YOU AGAIN SOON.

SINCERELY,
RICK JONES
(Redcatcher)

From: "Anderson Family"
Date: Fri, 21 Jun 2002

Patti,

Just read your book the other day. It was amazing. I never met your brother George, but now feel through your book that I knew him. Gave one to Faye and to Helen.

You did a wonderful job and I'm so proud of you.

Keep up the good work.
Ida Anderson
Cousin

Subject: Re: Hello
Tue, 25 Jun 2002

Hey Patti:

Great to hear from you... Good luck with the book. I'll check it out on Amazon. I live in Cinnaminson, NJ outside Philadelphia. My youngest goes into HS next year, so I'm a long way from retirement. I think of George often... mostly with Gag, boy were they funny! I'm in DC often and spend time at the Wall.

I'll pass the word about your book signing. Great picture of you... I'm sure I add very little.

Be Well...
Jack Peppard
My Friend

Hi Patti,

Jack Peppard, who I am in touch with forwarded me your e-mail. Would you send me the book and I will send you a check. Also perhaps Barbara Palowski could leave it with the Golf Pro or give it to me when she sees me at Roselle Golf Club.

I remember George. I am Viet Nam era Vet, retired from NJ Army National Guard. Never been in country but read a lot on the War.

I look forward to reading your book. What a celebrity you are!! My contact info is below.

Best,
Jim Scanlon 1965 LHS
Friend

Thu, 27 Jun 2002
Patti,

Thank you for mailing me the book. Tell me where to send the check. [I wish I was more familiar with how to order on Amazon] I read the reviews. I can't wait to read the book.

Robin Kornmeyer [1966] was a friend of Georges [he married Pat Smith. 1966]. I am in contact with them...Robin and George played baseball together and both had a St Elizabeth School or Church

connection. I too played ball with them .I will pass along all the info to Robin unless you already have his
Contact info.

Best,
Jim Scanlon LHS 65

Date: Wed, 10 Jul 2002 13:22:51 -0400
From: "Temples, Donna M
To: "Mom Enyedy

Mom,

WOW - I just finished your book over the weekend & I had to write to tell you how much I loved it & how proud I am of you for putting it out there to share with everyone. I can remember you telling me about your brother whenever the boys were just being too much boys for me to hang with and I'd spend time with you.

And of course now, all these years later it finally clicks for me on how you were the one who was able to help me move on after Dominick died. You already knew all about those special angels God needs because he already had your brother with him.

I'm sharing your book with my family and friends, and you again reminded me how very blessed I am and how much we need to live for the moment.

Thank you for sharing this with me. I hope all is well with you and the family. It was great to see you for those few minutes in the dance studio. Not sure if Elliott told you, but I also saw him at one of the Little League games. Seems your grandson is the same age as my new boyfriend's daughter who also plays ball. Yes - I have a new boyfriend who has custody of his 3 children. He's a great guy - very different from anyone I've ever known in my life. Not sure where it will lead, but I'm certainly enjoying every bit of it, and am glad to move on with my life.

Sorry to go on - I just wanted you to know that I love the book. And I'd love to send it up to you so I can have an autographed copy. Of course I'll have to get it back from my mom first.

Take care!!

Love,
Donna Temples
Friend of my son

Sent: Monday, July 29, 2002 5:06 PM

Patti,

I am not sure what to say. Except that I just found the web site for Redcatchers last week. In the message section I found a message from you about your brother. I do not want you to get overly excited but I served in D4/12 from June 68 to June 69 and may have known your brother. My name is Dan Foster and I knew of many guys with puppies (we kind of all adopted a puppy on occasions as we went through villages). I also remember having a monkey that we called Betty for a period of time.

Patti, 34 years is a long time. I have tried to forget much of what I saw and did over there. In fact I have had very little to do with the Army or most of the guy's I served with over there. Recently I had some cancer removed from my left ear. Many people stated that I should research Agent Orange. In doing so I researched the Redcatcher newsletter and the web page. I cannot remember your brother's name. Please do not be offended by that. I may not even remember his face if I were shown a picture. Time seems to remove some of what we saw and did years ago. I own a business and have a wonderful family here in San Diego.

I have not meant to forget my brothers in Nam. However I have learned over the years that most in this country are not even remotely interested in what we had to go through years ago. Rather than try to explain it to people I have chosen to provide the best I could for my family and maybe someday someone close to me would have an interest. If not I will continue to live my life the best I can. I started this note by saying that I wasn't sure what to say. You deserve to know someone that knew your brother over there. I just want to be very careful to not get your hopes up and to not give you the impression that I am some kind of crazy nut who wants to hurt you or anyone else. As stated I have stayed away from get togethers and only casual conversations over the years. I remember about 15 years ago some guys got together for my birthday. It was very scary to me because we all remembered different things and bringing it all back was uncomfortable to me.

Patti, I wish that I could clearly say that George and I were good friends. I lost a lot of good friends. When we first got to Nam they told us not to make friends. That making friends would only serve to cause great pain. We all suffered great pain anyway. Once again, I would love to be the Dan that your brother talked about in his letters. I may not be but we were in the same unit at the same time and could have run into each at one time or other. Bless your heart for thinking so much of your brother that you want to publish his letters. Would love to hear from you.

God Bless You,
Dan Foster
Redcatcher

From: Richard Toth
August 21, 2002 09:08:39
Subject: Knew your brother

Hi Pat,

Hope this letter finds you and your family in the best of everything. It's been a long time ago and if I remember right George and I had a class or two together. A very friendly guy. I sorry to hear of your loss. I too was in Nam with the Air Force, stationed in DaNang (69-70). My folks use to send me newspaper clippings from Linden about Viet Nam. Some good and some not good.

Another thing I remember is that you were a very attractive and bet you still are. Not going to the reunion this time, just to have a hot dog and to be at a ball park on the lower road of Linden. Until the next time take care and have a happy.

Richard Toth
Friend
PS: Say hello to everyone back East for me, Thanks

December 16, 2002

There is some information that you probably do not need to know, but I am sending it to you, because I sent it as a group. See below my previous contacts. I signed in the Redcatcher Web only 2 weeks ago. One of them might have known your brother.

JMFORTE
----- Original Message -----
From: JOSE FORTE
Sent: Tuesday, December 10, 2002 12:40 PM
Subject: J.M.FORTE / INFO.

Here it is:
Jose Manuel Forte

I was in Vietnam during Oct.31st, 1968 to October 30th 1969. I was trained in the U.S.A. to be in the Infantry. I was an 11C40 (Mortar Platoon). When I got to Vietnam, I was assigned to The 199th Lt. Inf. Brigade. Delta CO. / 4th Bn. / 12th Inf. Since there was no room for me at the 4th Platoon, I was put in the 2nd Pltn, where I stayed for approx. 7 months until I got in the 4th Pltn. I stayed with the 4th Pltn. until I made it back to U.S.A.

I was married when I went to Vietnam and remained married for over 35 years. We got divorced last January. I have two daughters, Maribel and Janette. They are very good girls.

After I left the military service, I continued to work and study at nights. It took me almost 7 years to graduate from College with a BS Degree in Industrial EngTech.. While I was still going to College, I got a job with Florida Power and Light. I worked in Power Plants for almost 2 years, until I was able to get in the Engineering Dpt. I was with FPL for approx. 20 years. I use to work as an Electrical Distribution Designer.

Right now I am on disability, due to the following. Over 2 years ago, my Doctor told me that I had pancreatic cancer and spreading to the liver. I have being under treatment since then, although I have been told by other Doctors that there is no cure for it. I am feeling a little better now and I hope that I last enough until something comes up. I do not worry about; I leave it up to God.
Well, enough about that.

Jose M. Forte

I am sorry for being boring, the worst is over.

THANKS,
J.M.Forte

December 16, 2002

Dear Patti:

I feel very happy for you, for being able to publish your book. At the same time I feel bad for being you the one who lost your brother. I can understand your feelings and the feelings of many other sisters, brothers, mothers, fathers and families who lost a relative there and at many other places of the World. I was a fortunate man to walk out of Vietnam alive, after being there for a whole year. I can tell you one thing, it has not been an easy task to forget what happened there and the young and brave men that I got to meet over there.

At age twenty-three, I was one of the oldest young men over there. I was already married, but I had no children. I was a little more mature, in a sense. I had some experience of what the Communism was starting to do to my country "Cuba". I left Cuba at age sixteen.

Going back to your brother, I was there during that time when he was hit by a land mine and with the same outfit. I knew many of the soldiers in my company, but mostly the ones in my platoon, because we used to be always together. At that time probably was the Second Platoon. I do not recall the names that well, but I do remember many faces. I do not remember his name but if I see a picture of him I might recognize him.

I will send you an e-mail with some information about myself and how you can contact me.

Thank you for contacting me and I hope to be of some help.

I would like to get more information about your book and where I could be able to get one.

Thanks again,
Your friend.

Jose M. Forte

December 17, 2002

Hello Patti:

Thank you for sending me your book. I will love to read it. I am a slow and lazy reader, but I definitely will let you know what I think of it. If I recognize your brother from the pictures, I will let you know too. I informed my daughter Janette about you and your work, and she was impressed and told me that she will also love to read your book. I will give her mine after I get done reading it. Thanks again and keep in touch.

Your friend,
Jose M. Forte

Jose passed away.

Feb 26 2003

Hello Brothers:

As you know I have been on a mission in writing my book on my brother George. I have found all of you and I am so grateful every day for my extended brothers.

I still have not found Glenn from VA, George's bunker buddy wounded 16 Mar 69 with severe feet injuries. My other mission is to find other families like ours and let them know how their loved ones were not forgotten. I would love to do something for us to correspond etc.

Is there anyway Glenn was not in the D4/12 if he was with George? I was reading George's letters yesterday and they both took so many pictures, I wonder if Glenn got his gear if he survived? Maybe he has the pictures of George, him and their puppy.

Any direction you can give me would be appreciated.

I love you all.
Patti

March 4, 2003

Patti,

I just received an email from Steve and was great to hear from him. We've been in touch by letters since last year's 199th reunion. I'm the Redcatcher that walked minimally with a full leg brace on my left leg and used a crutch. I bought your book and you signed it for me. We even spent a little time together talking and enjoyed our brief time together. At the services at the Wall I was in my wheelchair. It was a pleasure to meet you and you did a wonderful job on the book you wrote. I hope now that we'll have each other's email addresses we can keep in touch. Any chance you'll be at the reunion this year. I had a great time and met lots of guys I served with including two from my squad in Vietnam. This past year was the first we'd seen each other since then. It was a wonderful experience and this was only the second reunion I attended. The year before it was at Fort Benning, Georgia. As I told Steve, not long after the reunion I finally got a PC at home, but had no way of getting in touch with you. I hope now we can keep in contact a lot and look forward to seeing you again at another reunion soon. You have been in my thoughts often and was so glad we got to meet.

I've been battling Hepatitis C since 1992 when I was diagnosed with it. To date after four rounds of treatments it has not been put into remission. It was found that I got this from the many blood transfusions after my being wounded. I stopped this last therapy in Sept. 02, my body couldn't handle the treatments, which are a type of chemotherapy and is worse than the disease itself. I keep my hopes up that a better treatment or a cure is not far away. In the meantime things are getting worse as the Hep C picks up momentum and runs wild inside me.

Well, enough about me, I'll let you go and wait to hear from you soon. You take care, hope this finds you well and enjoying your weekend.

Your friend and a Redcatcher,

Dennis Haines

Date: Tue, 4 Mar 2003 20:58:07 EST
Subject: George and your book

Dear Pat,

Today I substituted at the high school. During my free period I went to the library to get a look at your book. It wasn't there. The librarian suggested I check with the History Department. Sure enough, they had the copies. They gave me one to read. (I still sent you the money for two, and I do want them.) Being in the History Department is a good place, because the students will be able to read the book.

Pat, I started reading the book in one of the classes, and I immediately couldn't stop the tears! Of course, I explained it to the students. Well, I just finished, and may I say it was/is wonderful. YOU HAVE DONE A MAGNIFICENT JOB. God Bless You!

All through these years I've thought of George frequently, and I've spoken about him to my family and others. I know I had a small child and was pregnant for my second during all of this and, of course, was worried about the war, etc. Too many were lost during that time. Friends of mine also never came home. But, George always stuck out in my mind. In the book people mention his smile...I, too, remember him that way. He was so very good-natured all the time. It was so nice to see the reflections of my former students, and the pictures were great reminders of the wonderful years gone by at LHS. You were among a great group of people in HS. Kids were respectful and family oriented. That is one of the reasons my husband and I chose to live in Linden. Your family must be so proud of you. I know that I'm proud to know you. This is truly a wonderful compliment to your family and brother and even to all those who were in Viet Nam. I hope you feel gratified in your tribute to George. You really should. Such a senseless loss of such a fine boy who became a man through such a difficult time.

My heart breaks for the ordeal you; your parents and family endured and still do. George was and still is a hero, and I will be sure to see that others are aware of this book if they aren't already.

Thank you again for calling. Please keep in touch and be well. I look forward to reading it again when I get my signed copy. I'm going to return this one when I'm back at the LHS.

With Love and Friendship,

Rita (Gallicchio) Greco (Mrs. G)
Our teacher in LHS

August 15, 2003

Dear President and Mrs. Bush:

First I want to say, I am honored to have you as our President and First Lady. You make us proud with your integrity and compassion to all Americans and the people around the world. There is no one else I would want to be leading us at this troubled time in our history.

Your father President Bush spoke at our son's commencement ceremony at Florida International University in 1992. He is wonderful and is a national treasure.

I am sending you a copy of my book, which was published, about **"my hero"** who died while serving his country in Vietnam. My brother George and I were so close and only 15 months apart in age. We looked like twins and felt like it too. I hope you enjoy my book. George was an average American boy sent to war and he served his country well.

I based my book around his letters he wrote home in those last 8 weeks of his life, those wonderful pieces of his heart. A "Redcatcher" is a soldier in the 199th Light Infantry Brigade. Last year I was invited by the 199th LIB to Washington on Memorial Day to participate in their Memorial Service at the Wall. I have been there many times but with his unit, it was so special and emotional. I read off George's name with pride. I had a book signing and met all my brother's comrades at their annual dinner that evening. The Redcatchers have adopted me and keep me in the loop. They are all extended family.

My book has sent me on a spiritual journey this past year. It has united old friends, touched people's souls that I don't even know and in ways I never imagined. It has given me confidence in myself at this time in my life being caregiver to our mother, blind with macular degeneration. She has lived to see her son honored in this wonderful way and remembered by so many after all these years.

May God Bless You in the days ahead. We are with you. I have a nephew deployed Major L.A. (Jack) McLaughlin; who inspired to publish my brother's letters. We are proud to have you as our Leader of the Free World.

Sincerely,

Patricia Farawell Enyedy

President and Mrs. Bush sent me Christmas cards from the White House.

March 20, 2003
Patti

I didn't read your e-mail as I responded before but I must tell I have been working on my book and had your book laying on my work table and as I went to put it away last night I had an overwhelming urge to help you find this Glenn. I then went through all the Redcatcher papers as well as e-mailed the historian and some Redcatchers asking for help as to searching for guys that had gotten a purple heart at that time they said the gov. won't let us find that out.

Patti I knew but not last night in all did I realize this was the day he had gotten wounded. I'm sure George was with me that last night.

Hope this is comforting to you.
Dennis

March 20, 2003

Ms. Jones,

My wife and I are both in favor of the showing of "The Long Way Home Project" and all of the others that are as well documented by the National Archives. It's long past due that our people should see the truth about Viet Nam. I fought there in 69-70 as an infantryman in the 199th Light Infantry Brigade in War Zone D. My wife Kim is a veteran of the Gulf War era. She was an Army medic.

"Silent Victory" is another documentary that should be aired. Don C Hall, formerly of the F51st LRPS (airborne) Infantry, and his wife, Annette Hall produced it with the help of other veterans including Norman Schwarzkopf. It was very well received at the Sedona Film Festival last month.

Thank you for your concern in efforts being made to set the records straight about the Viet Nam War.

Respectfully,
Rick and Kim Jones
Pittsburg, Texas

May 27, 2003

Dear Patti!

I am very proud to have served my Country in the Vietnam War, I served with Delta 4/12, 2nd platoon 199th Infantry brigade. I will always be a Redcatcher and proud to be one. I have been in contact with several other Redcatchers over the past few years. If it weren't for the internet this probably would not have happened! Some Redcatchers were not as fortunate as I, and made the ultimate sacrifice as your brother George did, and more than 58,000 others did in service of our Country. Not to mention the other Thousand's that were wounded and some disabled for life. We who served when our Country called upon us are brothers and will be always.

Patti as you know I bought your book that you wrote called (A Redcatchers letters from Nam) I knew George just for a short while, And it was an Honor to know him. After 35 years I can still see his face in my memory! Even before the book with his picture on the cover I remember the faces of all of the fallen comrades, even the ones that lived and died. It's just something that you never forget and don't want to. Thank God for all of our soldiers that served in all of the past wars and present.

God Bless the 199th, the ones who fought and died for Freedom,

Wayne Garrett
Served from October 1968 until October 1969.
Duncan, Oklahoma
May 27, 2003

Patti

I was in D troop 17th Cav. and a member of the 199th I have nothing but fond memories of this unit. The 199th was very well run and never did I witness any of the atrocities of war that many vets mention. The bad things people talk of in war did not happen in our unit and I'm proud of that.

I am still working on my book and have found that in writing this book I now that I've read the draft have been very much relieved and can now forget things I never thought I would. It seems as once I wrote it down and read it then I knew someone would know. Really can't explain it.

Your friend
Dennis

To: penyedy@yahoo.com

Dear Patty,

Hello to you and your family. I hope all are doing well. We are all fine here. I was wondering how I might be able to buy more copies of your book. Unfortunately, we only bought one, but it has sure traveled a lot! I would like to purchase 5 more because I want to make sure each of my children has one of their own and I am also trying to get one for my mom and one of my son's teachers. I have looked on 1stbooks.com but I can't find it there, so I am hoping you can help me.

Over the years, I have often encouraged my kids to bring the book to school when they were studying various things related to the Vietnam War. This year, Dustin, my youngest who is 12 years old, asked to bring it in to share with his class around Veterans Day. He proudly told me how six of his teachers each borrowed it and now one would like to buy it for his Dad. Robert and I were in the school for a conference tonight with 4 of Dustin's teachers and they all commented on how moving it is. See how many lives George - and you - have touched!

This past Memorial Day, Robert, Dustin and I went to Washington. We were mesmerized by Rolling Thunder and were honored to meet and talk with several Veterans. I was happy to see so many enjoying times together and the atmosphere seemed very positive. There were thousands of people cheering for them and they sure deserve it. We also visited The Wall and paid our respects to George. It is very important to Robert and me that our children learn about and hopefully someday understands the sacrifices others have made which enable them to live in freedom today.

Well, thanks for listening. Your brother George is the closest I have come to being connected to anyone who has fought in the Vietnam War, but I carry a deep respect for all who fought and feel a strong connection to them. Is it because it was the war of "my generation" or is it because I have just been open enough to stop and think about it - the suffering, sacrifice, dedication and valor? I'm not sure. I just know it is important.

Wishing you all a wonderful Thanksgiving. I hope to hear from you soon,

Love,
Anita (Ciano)
My cousin's wife

June 2 2,003

Patti,

I'm sorry you couldn't attend this year and you were missed. I did get to read your brother's name and also your remarks to the Brigade from your last email to me before the reunion. I was very honored and proud that I could do this for you. I sat next to Yolanda at the reading of the unit's killed in action. I went to the reunion this year with an Army buddy of mine from NY State. Ray was in my squad in Vietnam and the last we saw each other was the night of Dec. 5, 1968. I had to leave him and two other men from my squad behind to man the bunkers of our base camp perimeter. I would take the remainder of my squad and lead our entire Company on a night operation. In the very early hours of Dec. 6, that night I would be severely wounded and evacuated by helicopter to the 24th Evacuation Hospital at Long Bihn. I would never return that night and Ray and I would never meet again until Veterans Day 2002 at the 20th anniversary of the Vietnam Veterans Memorial. It was the most wonderful and emotional reunion ever for both of us. We first shook hands, then hugged and cried together. Ray was so relieved to see that I survived my wounds, but shocked at how they had left me paralyzed. I was just so glad to see him and know that he made it out of there alive. It was the very best reunion that one long overdue. Since that day we have been in touch a lot and will always be.

We made a vow to go together to the 199th reunion over the Memorial Day weekend this year. Ray drove down from NY Thursday and stayed at a motel close to me. Friday he picked me up and we headed to DC, arriving there around midafternoon. We signed in at the hospitality room, settled into our room and went for a nice meal. We pretty much just mingled with everybody there that day visited with a lot of the guys in the hotel lobby, hospitality room and back at our room. Saturday, the Brigade had a river boat cruise to Mount Vernon. We toured the mansion and had diner there and then ended our day at Arlington National Cemetery. Sunday, we placed cards of all our killed in action at each panel of the wall their name appeared on. At the reading of the Brigade KIA Ceremony, we read all 755 names of those killed in action. It was a very moving and emotional ceremony. I was honored to read the name of George T. Farawell this year.

After the unit's memorial service we stayed on Constitution Ave. for Rolling Thunder to come into town. Two and a half hours of nothing but motorcycles as far as you could see. That evening was the unit banquet at the Hotel and last time we were all together there. It all was the best of times and a wonderful four days. Monday, Memorial Day was the ceremony at the Vietnam Veterans Memorial. We arrived there very early for the reserved seating and one hour before the service, Nancy Sinatra sang for the full hour. She did songs that were appropriate for the day and the ceremony, but at the end of it sang what all of us wanted to hear her sing, "These boots were made for walking." Everyone stood up and cheered that she decided to sing this. The ceremony was nice afterwards and everything was exceptional. I got to personally meet Nancy Sinatra, we hugged, kissed and talked for a long while. What a wonderful lady and I also got her autograph. They had a special service at the Women's memorial, given by a Navaho Indian from Arizona. This was to honor the Indian girl killed in Iraq. Everything was so emotional. Ray and I stayed an extra night and headed home Tuesday. After dropping me off that evening he continued home, getting there very late that night. It was the very best reunion ever. Just when I think they can't be better, they are.

I know you'll do great at the dedication and I'm proud that you are an adopted Redcatcher and an excellent representative for us. Thanks again for becoming a good friend and only wish I could be there to see you do this. You take care and you'll be in my thoughts on this day. Have a good evening, write again soon and look forward to seeing you after the 4th of July.

A friend forever and Redcatcher,

Dennis Haines

VIETNAM ERA EDUCATIONAL CENTER HOSTS AUTHOR LECTURE

On Saturday, March 19, at 1:00 p.m., the New Jersey Vietnam Veterans' Memorial Foundation will host a lecture by Patricia Farawell Enyedy, author of A Redcatcher's Letters from Nam: Reflections of Family and Friends at the Vietnam Era Educational Center in Holmdel.

The author's brother, PFC George T. Farawell, was an average 19-year-old from a middle class family in Linden, New Jersey when he was drafted into the U.S. Army and shipped to Vietnam in 1969. The Army gave him an M16 and he was assigned to Delta Company, 4th Battalion, 12th Infantry Regiment of the 199th Light Infantry Brigade, known as the Redcatchers. He had served only eight weeks of his tour of duty when he fell victim to a land mine.

Patricia Farawell Enyedy, originally of Linden, NJ, writes, "My brother wrote 25 wonderful letters to my mom, dad, husband and myself. I was reading George's letters recently and thought no one else has ever read these wonderful pieces of his heart written during the last days of his life. I wanted to share them with family and his friends." Their reminiscences add to this poignant and brave profile of a soldier.

As a portrait of Farawell emerges from his sister's pages, we realize he is the boy next door, the sweetheart that will never come home, the brother and son that can never be replaced. Today the author lives in Carolina Shores, NC.

Lecture attendees are asked to RSVP to (732) 335-0033. A donation of $5.00 per person is suggested. The Vietnam Era Educational Center is located adjacent to the New

Jersey Vietnam Veterans' Memorial off the Garden State Parkway at exit 116. The Memorial and Educational Center are maintained through a partnership between the New Jersey Vietnam Veterans' Memorial Foundation and the New Jersey Department of Military and Veterans Affairs. The Educational Center is open Tuesday through Saturday, 10 AM – 4 PM. Regular admission is free for veterans and active-duty military personnel. Regular adult admission is $4.00; student and senior citizen admission is $2.00; and children under 10 are admitted free.

NJ Vietnam Veterans' Memorial Foundation

This is my speech I gave at the New Jersey Viet Nam Memorial in July 2003

Greeting

I would like to thank all of you for coming today. I am not a professional speaker so I am going to wing it and just chat. This is one of the best days of my life. I am glad you came to share it with me. Honoring George on his 36th Anniversary!!! 18 March 1969

I want to share with you the wonderful journey my book about "a boy" from Linden NJ has taken me on. I call George boy in my book because he was a boy, waving goodbye at Newark Airport, in Jan 1969, he was "our boy" going to war in a land he did not know. He was a man when he landed in Vietnam in the intense heat to meet his fate head on.

I am honored to be here today to speak in this "holy place". To experience this memorial with 1528 names of loved ones from our state of New Jersey is quite overwhelming. Every name on that black granite has a story just like ours.

Thank you Sibley Smith for your invitation to share my memories and my book, "A Redcatcher's Letters from Nam" about my brother PFC George Thomas Farawell from Linden, NJ who served in the US Army, 199th Light Infantry Brigade, Delta Company, 4th Battalion, 12th Infantry – 18 Jan to 18 March 1969.

How many people are here for the first time?

I would like to introduce you to:

My brother Stephen lives in Elizabeth and he had really big boots to fill all these years after losing his best buddy. He was a senior in high school in 1969.

My daughter Amanda and son-in-law Bill La Grutta who live in Rochester, NH.

My son Elliott, his wife Mary Beth and my grandchildren Tyler and Courtney from Hillsborough NJ.

George's friends who are here today Richard, Jennifer and Natalie Gagliardi to those who wrote reflections and those who wanted to be here today, thank you from the bottom of my heart.

Family and friends who are here thank you for coming you know how deeply I love you.

Two people are missing today

My husband Elliott of 35 years who has lived with me through tears and laughter; He encourages me to follow my dream and then is amazed when I do. He had to tell me, as a newlywed that George was gone and I said gone where? He said think of the baby. George is dead. It was the first time in my life I had to face grief in such a degree that I wanted to scream and I did.

Missing today is my mother, Mary. She has been my inspiration my whole life of what a mother and friend should be. She was 90 in October. I watched how strong this woman had to be in March of 1969. She dealt not only with her overwhelming grief with the death of "her boy" but my dad's grief, my brother Stephen's grief and mine. I was told the day before I was pregnant with her first grandchild. She is the epitome of grace and loyalty. I am proud to call her 'mother".

Thank Veterans

I would also like to take this opportunity to thank all veterans in the audience, please stand up and let us give you a big thank you.

The Vietnam War was such a part of my life and I realized my kids did not know anything about their uncle or learn about the war in school that also inspired me to do something.

I am very proud my book is reading material in the history department in Linden High School where we graduated.

Opening

We were here for the dedication of this memorial 10 years ago as "Gold Family" with Gov. Christi Todd Whitman and General Norman Schwarzkopf in attendance along with honor guards from all branches of the military from across the state.

That beautiful Sunday in April was packed with so much emotion I think then was when I started thinking about "all veterans".

In my mind George never aged and to see middle-aged veterans saying thank you and crying as we passed in the procession

If you had told me I would write a book and be standing here 5 years ago I would have said NO WAY! It is something I always wanted to do but had no confidence to try it.

In March 2001, I was reading my brother's letters he wrote from Vietnam and thought one had ever read these wonderful pieces of his heart.

In April 2001, my nephew Major Jack McLaughlin US 3rd Calvary who is not here today, he left for his 2nd tour in Iraq on 3/06/05 **asked me if he could read one of George's**

letters and told me what an elite unit the 199th Light Infantry Brigade was. He encouraged me to write my book.

I had to get my thoughts together, where would I start?

The letters, maybe I could find Glenn after all these years? Could I find all of his friends to write something for the book, where are they and how did they find out. What are they doing now?

One of George and mine best friends Richard Gagliardi was coming for a visit with his wife Jennifer. I told them of my wish and they read the letters that weekend. With their encouragement and commitment to write "reflections" of their friend my journey began...................

Redcatcher's

I had lots of homework to do including finding veterans in the 199th LIB. I posted my name on the website and that same day Clay Crowder contacted me telling me George was a fellow Redcatcher and could he please honor him on his website. The rest is history.

Word got out that I was looking for anyone who remembered George from the Delta 4/12 and one by one they wrote me. Some not right away they have to deal with their memories again and hopefully say the right words to the families.

The 199th Light Infantry Brigade as a fellow "Redcatcher Sister" has adopted me.

These remarkable men who have had to live with so many horrible memories went on to live their lives to the fullest with some good days and many bad days but always moving on. Tomorrow will be better.

They still give each other moral support and are still finding their brothers today! They recently found Jose Forte in Florida. He is battling cancer but the brothers got him involved looking up pictures etc. In a few weeks there is a spark in his emails. I know one of these days I will see my brother in one of their pictures.

As my book was read by the Redcatcher's one by one they wrote me, they were there with George in his daily words written at the side of the river, building 2 man bunkers etc. **but many cannot remember his face.**

One Redcatcher knew it was George by his smile and had a story to tell me. They returned from an ambush and were out for a few days so food was dropped in for dinner. **They had steak for the first time,** which was a real treat. George was sad that day did not feel like eating. He gave me his steak and said "Happy Birthday" and smiled that smile of his. He never forgot that act of kindness on that March day in 1969.

The 199th LIB they did all foot patrol. George wore out a pair of boots in a month. Wayne Garrett from OK remembers George and he did not know George died after he was transported at night to the hospital after stepping on a land mine. He had severe shoulder and stomach injuries. **The vets who made through their whole tour are forever brothers,** the **KIA's are brothers with no face but they are etched forever in their hearts**.

The Redcatcher's honor their dead in Washington at the Vietnam Wall in DC every memorial day, every 5 years at Ft. Benning GA. Some have written books, magazine articles, etc. Some need to be in touch with others while others cannot bear it. Dealing with the aftermath of war is a personal thing for each.

I dropped my manuscript in the mail and went on vacation on 9/8/01 to Myrtle Beach. Yes, that horrible week of 9/11 forever etched in our minds and hearts. In the back of my mind, I kept thinking how my little book would be accepted with this going on.

Little did I realize how my little book about a Vietnam Vet would make such an impact on my life?

I found 1st Books on the Internet and they print on demand. My husband Elliott's customers in graphic design designed the beautiful cover and those are George's real envelopes addressed to my mom. To see the first copy of my book it was so emotional. I cried and I cried and I laughed and was so damn proud of myself for fulfilling my dream and hoping I made my brother proud.

I did a live talk radio show from NC with Ken Bagwell of Heads up America. I was nervous at first but Ken put me at ease immediately and it went great......... He used my book as a lead in for the Memorial Day Weekend, 3 Redcatcher's called in to comment.

The Redcatcher's invited me to Washington DC in 2002 to participate with the Redcatcher's Memorial at the Wall on Memorial Day. To try and put into words the trip to DC, it was awesome... More gratifying than I ever imagined.

Sunday morning we went to the Vietnam Memorial Wall where cards are placed on each of the 715 KIA from the 199th LIB. We then went to a grassy knoll where veterans read all the 715 names.

I was asked to read George's name and say something if I wanted. I read the dedication from my book and told them that a year ago; I did not know what a Redcatcher was; and now I have all this extended family. Another sister was there also. Yolanda spoke and **we both carried the wreath to the center of the monument for the dedication.**

I had a book signing that night at the dinner and one by one they came to buy a book and thank me............ for what I have done for the Redcatcher's..............

They each hugged me and cried, all of them.

I **met the Lt. who put George on the chopper and his Sgt. at the time.**

I met Dennis a farmer from MN who wants to write a book,

Ram from TX who was the medic,

Poncho from CA who has a website and George is on it.

Jeff Voorhees from Horseheads NY not far from where my husband was born.

Dennis Haines from PA who has become a great friend,

We met families of other vets

I was presented a plaque with the inscription "Patricia Enyedy Redcatcher's Award for Writing Excellence" I was stunned and the tears flowed

Also given the award was Bob Fromme who helped me so much in finding people and guiding me. We had a wonderful talk and I made so many new friends.

One thing, I still have not found Glenn his bunker buddy he writes about in his letters. Sometimes I think he was an angel.

I would like to share with you some words from the Redcatcher's Letters

May 2, 2002

PATTI,

I RECEIVED THE BOOK THIS AFTER AND COULDN'T PUT IT DOWN TILL I FINISHED IT.

THOSE EIGHT WEEKS WERE A LIFETIME TO GEORGE EVEN THOUGH HE KEPT THEM CALM AND COLLECTED IN HIS LETTERS.

HE WAS JUST AS ALL OF US GRUNTS WERE IN DELTA COMPANY; ALWAYS GLAD TO SEE THE SUNRISE THE NEXT DAY.

GEORGE, BY ALL THAT I KNOW AND BELIEVE, WAS A VERY HONORABLE "BOY" THAT WAS CAUGHT UP INTO THE TRAP THAT SO MANY HAD TO TRY TO ENDURE DURING THAT TERRIBLE WAR.

I ADMIT THAT I CRIED ALL THE WAY THRU THE BOOK AND WILL AGAIN WHEN I REREAD IT. I'M SURE I WILL READ IT COUNTLESS TIMES BECAUSE I HAD ALL OF THOSE FEELINGS THAT GEORGE EXPRESSED IN HIS LETTERS AND THOSE I KNEW HE WAS FEELING WITHOUT PUTTING THEM INTO WORDS. HE WAS ALWAYS SCARED AS WE ALL WERE. FEAR KEPT US ALIVE AS LONG AS FATE AND LUCK RAN WITH US AS INDIVIDUALS. WE ALL HAD A NUMBER AND GEORGE'S WAS CALLED THAT DAY IN MARCH 1969.

THANKS TO MEN LIKE HIM THE UNIT GAINED MORE INTELLIGENCE, CUNNING AND A BIGGER REASON FOR "PAYBACK" TO MAKE UP, IN OUR MINDS, A REASON TO CARRY ON.

THANK YOU SO MUCH FOR SHARING GEORGE'S LETTERS WITH ALL BECAUSE THEY MEAN EVERYTHING TO A VIETNAM VETERAN THAT GOT EVEN CLOSE TO COMBAT. MY LOVE TO YOU AND ALL YOUR FAMILY,

RICKY W. JONES,

Dear Patti!

I am very proud to have served my Country in the Vietnam War; I served with Delta 4/12, 2nd platoon 199th Infantry brigade. I will always be a Redcatcher and proud to be one. I have been in contact with several other Redcatcher's over the past few years. If it weren't for the Internet this probably would not have happened! Some Redcatcher's were not as fortunate as I, and made the ultimate sacrifice as your brother George did, and more than 58,000 others did in service of our Country. Not to mention the thousand's that were wounded and some disabled for life.

We who served when our Country called upon us are brothers and will be always. Patti as you know I bought your book that you wrote called (A Redcatcher's letters from Nam) I knew George just for a short while, **and it was an Honor to know him. After 35 years I can still see his face in my memory!** Even before the book with his picture on the cover I remember the faces of all of the fallen comrades, even the ones that lived and died. It's just something that you never forget and don't want to. Thank God for all of our soldiers that served in all of the past wars and present.

God Bless the 199th, the ones who fought and died for Freedom,
Wayne Garrett, Served from October 1968 until October 1969.
Duncan, Oklahoma

Dear Patti:
I feel very happy for you, for being able to publish your book. At the same time I feel bad for being you the one who lost your brother. I can understand your feelings and the feelings of many other sisters, brothers, mothers, fathers and families who lost a relative there and at many other places of the World. I was a fortunate man to walk out of Vietnam alive, after being there for a whole year. I can tell you one thing, it has not been an easy task to forget what happened there and the young and brave men that I got to meet over there.

At age twenty-three, I was one of the oldest young men over there. I was already married, but I had no children. I was a little more mature, in a sense. I had some experience of what the Communism was starting to do to my country "Cuba". I left Cuba at age sixteen.

Going back to your brother, I was there during that time when he was hit by a land mine and with the same outfit. I knew many of the soldiers in my company, but mostly the ones in my platoon, because we used to be always together. At that time probably was the Second Platoon. I do not recall the names that well, but I do remember many faces. I do not remember his name but if I see a picture of him I might recognize him.

Thank you for contacting me and I hope to be of some help.

Thanks again,
Your friend,
Jose M. Forte Redcatcher
DECEASED

> **I wish I could reach more families like myself to let them know all that still goes on in their loved one's memory with websites, books, magazine articles, etc.**
> Poncho wrote me after reading my book after Memorial Day last year, that they could have been his letters. **"All they all wanted to do was go home, and George was one of the one "to go home early."**

His Friends

> **I have reunited with all of our old friends.** They have supported me by **finding each other** and **writing heartwarming reflections of their friend.**
> **Emotions buried for years surface and we are young again.** Most of George's friends were in the military too. I am glad to say they returned to live wonderful productive lives and lived "for their friend". I am proud of each of them. I know coming to grips with their feelings again in middle age was worth it. We laughed and cried and the stories flowed.

I have enough Material for another book and I am keeping all of the "Reflections

To Remember" for my children and grandchildren.
I am still hearing from childhood and high school friends and teachers some I don't remember but they are compelled to write and I love it.

I read every letter to my mother who has macular degeneration now and has no central vision. She is amazed how many remember her boy and I am finally at peace with his passing.

A letter from Bill Margel (closing paragraph of Steve's friend)

I'll close with my most vivid memory of George. It was probably mid to late spring. I remember being at the park, probably playing basketball. George came striding into the park from Bergen Ave. He had on his Linden High Varsity jacket, a pair of tan work pants and high top sneakers. I remember his short blond hair and a big smile. I remember him a grabbing basketball and said, "Let's play."

My Friend

My brother was such a big part of my life. We were like twins in our early years we were always together. We slept in the same room until we moved to Linden (we thought it was the country) I wanted my kids and grandkids to know something about their Uncle and a war that was not taught in school.

I was trying to think of a comparison for our children to realize how far we have come and I want to tell them, **none of my grandparents could read or write.**

Days in the 50's and 60's were simpler then. **We were all the same, went to school, came home, changed your clothes and ran out the door to play. All we needed to**

play was a ball of some kind. There were no lessons etc. because there was no extra money. We got one pair of sneakers a year, I have a picture of George and the basketball team all had on different shorts and the sneakers had holes in them and some had on black shoes. We attended St. Elizabeth's School in Linden, NJ and all graduated from Linden High School.

There was no cable, computers, internet, instant replay, mom did not work, we had 1 car in the driveway with a stick shift on the column which most of us learned to drive on, a black and white TV (color in high school). When George left for Nam he bought my parents a stereo hi-fi for the living room. He loved Bill Cosby. We would sit as a family and laugh again and again at Fat Albert.

In his short life, I can't believe how people still remember George after all these years. One veteran found me and told me he thinks he remembers George, not by name but by his smile. I have heard from so many people about his smile. **When George was very young he had buckteeth and my mom went to work part time to pay for his braces. When they came off he smiled all the time and by then no one would dare call him Bucky Beaver again.**

He was tough and strong, tender and loving, funny and serious. He excelled in any sport he played from Linden PAL Basketball and Baseball, St Elizabeth's CYO basketball, Linden HS baseball and the Betsytown county league.

George also was an **excellent bowler.** Jersey Lanes was his second home along his friends. In those days you could hitchhike a ride down Elizabeth Ave. to the "alleys". George and his friends had the run of the place.

They have told me so many wonderful funny stories of those days.

They never got in trouble or did anything wrong:

Well maybe some drinking,
Did I say underage drinking?
Hanging out at Denino's in Staten Island playing pool
Driving home tipsy with no designated driver
They told me that was before it became
the law not to drink and drive,
Or
Hiding behind the beer cooler at the alleys and
Swiping Buds while sitting on the floor.
Hiding behind the jukebox while they locked up for the night.
After it closed they bowled only in the middle lanes so
The cops could not see them in their security checks.
And driving their cars into
The alleys through the front door
They did not damage anything or hit anyone.
Mike Favor drove his new Harley in the alleys
Last year at my book signing it was just like the old days!
They never had any confrontations:
Maybe some shoving and pushing, some name-calling
Maybe a couple of fights, they never looked for trouble
It found them!
(George was the protector of all of his friends
and me)
And a few other things like:
Some card playing and gambling,
Starting a valet service parking cars at the alleys and
No one had a license!
Calling home at 3:00 in the morning saying
Tell Dad I am going to be Late!
All good clean fun!

Today

I hope you all realize you have lived your life for George and all the deceased veterans. It is their duty to keep our freedom and they did.

You are free. Yes, freedom is alive.

We must stand behind our wonderful President who by the way I sent my book to. He and Mrs. Bush sent me back a hand signed note. It is in the lobby.

Our technology in our military today is quite different, as we have witnessed in the war in Iraq.

These men and women are trained professionals.

They each have a job to perform to keep the precision clock ticking.

They can perform surgery in a tent set up in 2 hrs. with a full operating room.

They can build a bridge in a matter of hours.

They can rescue a private in the middle of the night with only the word of a doctor trying to help an American prisoner like Jessica Lynch.

In closing, take a minute to ask yourself if you have accomplished all you wanted to do?

Is there something you missed and wish you could go back? Try it again - don't wait another minute.

Go out tomorrow and plant that seed.

Every day you live should be a memorial, a landmark of appreciation, known and shown, not taken lightly.

Reach out to thank a veteran, help someone in need, call someone you miss, forgive someone, contact old friends, they do want to hear from you again. I have learned that in my journey.

Because in the blink of an eye we are middle aged!

How could time possible pass so quickly?

Go leave your mark on the world……………………

From: Robert. Gouge
To: penyedy@yahoo.com
Subject: 199ᵗʰ Inf. Bed. Vietnam

Patricia,

My name is Robby Gouge and I am a historian and secondary education teacher in Asheville, North Carolina. The purpose of this email deals with the 199ᵗʰ Light Infantry Brigade in Vietnam. (If you are wondering how I got your Email address, I read your book and noticed it was listed on p. 63).

Several weeks ago, I purchased "**A Redcatcher's Letters from Nam"** and wanted to commend you on a wonderful and touching book and for keeping the memory of your brother, George, alive. He is and always will be a true American hero and his sacrifice will never be forgotten. (My father also served in the 199ᵗʰ in Vietnam during his tour from 1969-1970, although he was not in the same battalion as your brother). I am also pleased to make your acquaintance.

For nearly twenty-five years, I have been a serious student of the Vietnam War and have devoted much of my spare time to studying about the history and men of the 199ᵗʰ Inf. Bed. During this time, I have gathered a significant bit of information on the unit while in Vietnam and have conducted many interviews with area veterans from eastern Tennessee and western North Carolina who served in the unit from 1966-1970. While meeting with these veterans, a common theme among them has been the question, "Why can I not find any books about our unit in Vietnam and why is the history of our unit always overlooked?" As you know, there is little if anything out there in the mainstream media on the Redcatcher's of the 199ᵗʰ.

When I started this project, it was for my own research, curiosity, and enjoyment. However, my interest has grown and like you, I have the great desire to one day publish a book. This is not something that I expect to see on every bookshelf in every bookstore. Instead, this is something that I feel I need to do, as my small and humble tribute to the Redcatcher's of the 199th LIB, so their stories and sacrifices will never be forgotten. In short, and just like your book, it is time the men of the 199th received some long overdue Recognition, albeit thirty-five years after the fact.

This work would be about the history (although not a definitive one) on the 199th LIB while in Vietnam, with a major emphasis on the first-hand experiences of the veterans who served in the unit, specifically the ones that I have interviewed.

Even though I work on this project in my spare time and it is far from completion, I wanted to ask about the publishing process, specifically about 1st Book publishers, and see how it is done as I am in the dark about the whole process.

How do you start? What do you do? Cost? What pointers and advice do you have?

I would appreciate any help and suggestions that you could provide.

Thanks for your time and have a blessed day.

Sincerely,

Robby Gouge
Asheville, NC

To:	"Patti Enyedy" <penyedy@yahoo.com>
Subject:	Re: 199th Inf. Bde., Vietnam

Patti,

Thank you so much for your reply and what a small world! I live approx. 15 minutes north of Asheville and the Biltmore Estate and listen occasionally to Bagwell's show while driving to school in the mornings.

It would be a pleasure to try and meet with you in the future. Please keep me informed of your plans as we could surely work something out.

To answer your question, my father, Jack Gouge (he turned 56 this past April) was a 22 year old draftee and college graduate who ended up serving in Headquarters and Headquarters Company, 199th, from July of 1969 to February of 1970. My father saw quite a bit of the Vietnamese countryside (and action) as he was, most of the time, a jeep driver for the Brigade S-1 and S-2. His duties took him to nearly all of the 199th's base camps, firebases and forward areas at one time or another. He also had the opportunity to see many of the 199th's officers and men because he was in HHC. Because he was at the right place at the right time, he became the first enlisted member of the Redcatchers Association while in Vietnam. (Of further interest, three of his high-school classmates were also drafted together in 1968 and all served with the 199th from 69-70 as well).

Interestingly, there are 15-20 or more 199th veterans in the east Tennessee and Western North Carolina area and I have had the pleasure and honor of interviewing most of them over the past couple of years. It is their stories and memories that I want to preserve and write about. They deserve it. The 199th LIB also deserves to be better known as there are countless deeds and achievements that were done by the unit and the men in Vietnam (such as Chaplain Liteky, Gen. Davison, Gen. Bond and many others.

Being a historian, I have had the opportunity to go to many places and conduct research, but I have always come up empty handed most of the time when trying to find specific information on the 199th. I even have a close colleague of mine who is a Military History instructor for the Infantry Officers Candidate School at Fort Benning, Georgia who tells me there is very little information on the unit located in the Infantry Archives/Records at the Ft. Benning Donovan Research Library. What a shame! (However, there is an excellent Display dealing with the 199th at the Infantry Museum).

I am very excited to hear that there are more upcoming projects dealing with the 199th and its history and am eager to see them when they come out.

Thanks and I look forward to hearing from you again. Also, I hope you begin to feel better soon! God bless.

Sincerely,

Robby Gouge

November 1, 2003

SUBJECT:
RE: THANK YOU VETERANS

Patti,
Thank you so much for being such a care-giver to a silent Group, the Veterans themselves (myself included). Wasn't till recently that I discussed or spoke proudly of being a Vet...It's people like yourself that deserve allot of credit for the positive image you give The Veteran...Thank you again

Sincerely,
Mark Donaldson

Date: Thu, 19 Feb 2004

Date: Thu, 10 Jun 2004 10:27:45 -0700
From:
"Wayne Nicholls"
To: penyedy@yahoo.com
Subject: Redcatcher Sister

Dear Patti,

Thank you for sending a note and wonderful tribute to George. I wrote you a letter and enclosed a couple photos.

Debbie flew to Washington D.C. to meet me in my pilgrimage to the Wall. We had an awesome and emotional journey. It was a great honor to meet you, my fellow Redcatchers and other Vietnam Veterans. The Redcatcher Reunion Family Buffet was one of the highlights of our journey with the "Run For The Wall".

We left Alexandria, VA on Tuesday morning and arrived (via motorcycle) in Long Beach at 1:00 AM Saturday morning. The trip was very emotional and a sense of healing to this old Vietnam Vet. It was a true "Welcome Home" all the way across this great nation.

Thank you again!
God Bless you and our Redcatcher family.

Wayne

Wayne Nicholls

Friday, June 25, 2004

FRIENDS RUN FOR THE WALL, PART II

By Wayne Nicholls

On May 19, 2004, Steven H. Neal, Terry Byrnes and I (all Long Beach natives) left Ontario, CA with over 300 other bikers to Washington, D.C. with "Run For The Wall". The mission of the RFTW is to create a groundswell of support for American PRISIONERS OF WAR and MISSING IN ACTION from all wars, and to help those injured by war to heal. Traveling by motorcycle, the three of us carried the names of 103 Long Beach area soldiers who died or MIA in Vietnam.

Terry served in the military at home while Steven and I both had tours in Vietnam. Those who went to Vietnam, usually went there alone without benefit of going with a group. Likewise, we came home alone. More often than not, the G.I. experienced an unfavorable greeting by War Protesters. There were no "pat-on-the-back, how-do-you-do, or welcome home". We returned with a mixed bag of feelings about the war in Vietnam and our own personal involvement. Yet those of us lucky enough to return were often disappointed and labeled by the Americans we had served.

Thirty-plus years later, on the first day of this 10-day organized ride across America, we discovered an added personal benefit of being part of the RFTW group. We received a true "Welcome Home" that continued all the way across this great nation. Americans, all sizes, shapes and colors, young, old, veterans and non-veterans lined many of the city streets and freeway overpasses with American and POW-MIA flags, waiving, saluting, most yelling "Welcome Home!" For the first time, it was "okay to be a Vietnam Veteran" and for many, including the three of us, it became an emotional and healing journey.

There was much celebration as we arrived in Washington, D.C. We would assemble at the Jefferson Monument for a group picture. Ride to Arlington National Cemetery and lay a flower reef at the Tomb of the Unknown. Visit the Korean War and World War II Memorials, and to complete our journey, deliver the names of our Long Beach hero's to the Wall.

It was Terry's and my first visit to the Vietnam Veterans Memorial. Although I knew it was something I had to do, it presented me with a challenge to muster-up the courage to go. We decided to go there the following day, without the RFTW group and with our wives who had flown over to join us.

Terry, Steven and I each had a binder. On the cover was a color picture of the Long Beach Vietnam Veterans Memorial. Inside listed all 103 Long Beach area KIA & MIA's. Also added to the list was Steven's brother-in-law, Joseph M. Romero killed in action in 1968. He was a Long Beach boy, but since his parents moved to Lakewood while he was in Vietnam, his name is not included on the Long Beach memorial.

At the base of the Wall, I viewed the 199th Light Infantry Brigade remembrance cards for each of the 755 KIA/MIA's during its deployment to Vietnam from 1966 to 1970. I had served with the 199th L.I.B. in Vietnam during 1970. I made it a point to visit five names I felt important for me to see. Three of those were childhood friends including Joey, Rodney Little and Christopher Kurtz. With tears in my eyes, I paused to remember their young faces. I thanked them and prayed that someday we would meet again. I placed the binder at the base of Christopher's panel. From there, it will be cataloged and placed in a future constructed museum that will house millions of items left at the Vietnam Veterans Memorial. Leaving our binders, our mission with "Run For The Wall" was completed. It had been an awesome, healing and rewarding experience.

Date: Thu, 23 Sep 2004 08:47:59 -0700
From: "Wayne Nicholls"
To: "Patti Enyedy" <penyedy@yahoo.com>

Hello Patti,

The last weekend of September is set aside to honor our Gold Star Mothers. This Sunday, I am riding with a group of local RFTW bikers to the Gold Star Manor, here in Long Beach, CA. When originally dedicated, the Gold Star Manor housed over 300 Gold Star Mom's from all wars.

Since the end of the Vietnam War, this number has dropped to around 10. Unfortunately, with our current involvement in Iraq and elsewhere, the number of new Gold Star Mother's is growing.

Along with us on our Sunday visit to Gold Star Manor, we'll be taking cookies, donuts, corsages and plenty of hugs to remind these honorable women know that they are not forgotten.

God Bless your Gold Star family!

Wayne
B 2/40 - 199th LIB
1970

Wayne Nicholls
Gold Star Mother's Day
Sunday, September 26, 2004
Wayne Nicholls, Vietnam Veteran

Sunday morning I put the American flag on the front porch next to the MIA-POW flag I fly 24/7. It was a very special day, one that several of my neighbors needed to be reminded of. It was "Gold Star Mother's Day".

RFTW Brother Danny Lopresto had coordinated a ride to the "Gold Star Manor" in Long Beach, California. Most years, they have a big celebration at the retirement home. This year, nothing was planned. Hearing that, Danny contacted some of the local RFTW participants to gather and let our Gold Star Mother's know that they are not forgotten. Most riders met a "Fingers" house at 11:00 AM for the ride to Long Beach. RFTW Brother Steven Neal and I, along with our wives, decided that we'd meet the group there.

It was a wonderful feeling to see some of our Brothers being led by Danny and "Fingers" riding in formation. When they entered the gated property, we joined them in parade to our designated parking area. Greetings and hugs were plentiful as we gathered for our "group picture" and "rider's meeting".

Danny explained the history of Gold Star Mothers, dating back to WWI when families of soldiers would display a blue star in their windows representing their child's service. When news came that their child had been killed, a Gold Star was placed over the blue one. In 1938, the President signed a proclamation, declaring the last Sunday in September as "Gold Star Mother's Day". Gold Star Manor in Long Beach (one of two dedicated facilities) had originally provided residence to 300+ Gold Star Mothers. Since the end of the Vietnam War, the number has dropped to less than 10. Unfortunately with our involvement with the war on Terrorism, the number of Gold Star Mothers will increase. Danny had made arrangements to visit and have lunch with the remaining Moms. Ed "Fingers" and Lisa brought along beautiful corsages for each of these honorable women.

Jim "Jumper" Braga, 2005 RFTW State Coordinator, provided a warm and heartfelt introduction of the "Run For The Wall"; who we are, what we do, and a very special, sincere thank you to the "Gold Star Mom's" (and one "Gold Star Dad) that had given the ultimate sacrifice for our freedom.

Then one of the Mothers stood to say, "Thank you, it is so nice to know that we are not forgotten" and she added that not a day passes without thinking about her child and it is nice to know he too is being honored. She had brought tears to our eyes. It had been a wonderful day and another rewarding experience with the Brotherhood of Run for the Wall.

During the 2005 RFTW, we will carry the names of their sons with us to the Wall as we travel across this great nation.

November 1, 2003

Subject:
Re: Thank you Veterans

Patti,
Thank you so much for being such a care-giver to a silent Group, the Veterans themselves (myself included). Wasn't till recently that I discussed or spoke proudly of being a Vet...It's people like yourself that deserve allot of credit for the positive image you give The Veteran...Thank you again

Sincerely,
Mark Donaldson

Date: Thu, 10 Jun 2004 10:27:45 -0700
From: "Wayne Nicholls
To: penyedy@yahoo.com
Subject: Redcatcher Sister

Dear Patti,

Thank you for sending a note and wonderful tribute to George. I wrote you a letter and enclosed a couple photos.

Debbie flew to Washington D.C. to meet me in my pilgrimage to the Wall. We had an awesome and emotional journey. It was a great honor to meet you, my fellow Redcatchers and other Vietnam Veterans. The Redcatcher Reunion Family Buffet was one of the highlights of our journey with the "Run For The Wall".

We left Alexandria, VA on Tuesday morning and arrived (via motorcycle) in Long Beach at 1:00 AM Saturday morning. The trip was very emotional and a sense of healing to this old Vietnam Vet. It was a true "Welcome Home" all the way across this great nation.

Thank you again!
God Bless you and our Redcatcher family.

Wayne

Wayne Nicholls

Friday, June 25, 2004

Date:	Tue, 20 Nov 2007 23:19:43 EST
Subject:	Happy Thanksgiving!
To:	penyedy@yahoo.com

Dear Patty,

Hello to you and your family. I hope all are doing well. We are all fine here. I was wondering how I might be able to buy more copies of your book. Unfortunately, we only bought one, but it has sure traveled allot! I would like to purchase 5 more because I want to make sure each of my children has one of their own and I am also trying to get one for my mom and one of my son's teachers. I have looked on 1stbooks.com but I can't find it there, so I am hoping you can help me.

Over the years, I have often encouraged my kids to bring the book to school when they were studying various things related to the Vietnam War. This year, Dustin, my youngest who is 12 years old, asked to bring it in to share with his class around Veterans Day. He proudly told me how six of his teachers each borrowed it and now one would like to buy it for his Dad. Robert and I were in the school for a conference tonight with 4 of Dustin's teachers and they all commented on how moving it is. See how many lives George - and you - have touched!

This past Memorial Day, Robert, Dustin and I went to Washington. We were mesmerized by Rolling Thunder and were honored to meet and talk with several Veterans. I was happy to see so many enjoying time together and the atmosphere seemed very positive. There were thousands of people cheering for them and they sure deserve it. We also visited The Wall and paid our respects to George. It is very important to Robert and me that our children learn about and hopefully someday understand the sacrifices others have made which enable them to live in freedom today.

Well, thanks for listening. Your brother George is the closest I have come to being connected to anyone who has fought in the Vietnam War, but I carry a deep respect for all who fought and feel a strong connection to them. Is it because it was the war of "my generation" or is it because I have just been open enough to stop and think about it - the suffering, sacrifice, dedication and valor? I'm not sure. I just know it is important.

Wishing you all a wonderful Thanksgiving. I hope to hear from you soon,

Love,
Anita (Ciano)

6/12/09

Patty - These are two editorials I wrote a while ago. Forgive me if I've already sent these. The older I get, the more I repeat myself.

Support our returning troops

There is a tragedy being perpetuated regarding our returning troops, which remains under the radar to many. This concerns helping them put their personal lives back in order. Many politicians support our troops in combat, or say they do when it serves their political purpose, but this support is glaringly negligent when the soldiers return home. Our brave men and women endure monumental hardships in battle, that we can only try to imagine. Meanwhile, their families endure other hardships on the homefront, exacerbated by the effects of injuries, family stress and financial problems. I personally know of several such cases.

There will always be debate regarding the wisdom and necessity of any war, but there can be no debate regarding the debt we owe our returning heroes. Veterans are not looking for a handout, but they deserve all the assistance America can give them. Countless private organizations and individual citizens make a tremendous effort to help with their time and money, but there is still a glaring deficiency, whose solution must fall on the shoulders of Congress. Politicians vote themselves obscene salaries and pensions, while many veterans struggle to adjust and make ends meet. I propose a novel idea. Divert the funding we lavish upon illegal immigrants toward providing better lives for the volunteer defenders of this country.

Since Congress holds the purse strings, they have the authority and the moral obligation to do the right thing. Mark Twain wrote " Patriots always love and respect their country, and their government when it deserves it." In this instance, our government deserves neither.

Don Maresca Sun City

<u>Some old wounds never heal.</u>

Patty - I got some interesting feedback on this one. The editor said her dad is a Vietnam veteran and she had tears in her eyes when she was reading it. She showed it to her dad, and it was one of the few times she saw him cry. I also got some phone calls from wives, even one visiting from Tennessee, who said it brought tears to their husbands eyes and thanked me for writing it. It was something that had to be said, and was long overdue. This is what makes writing these worthwhile.

My wife and I were recently in the Savannah Airport awaiting our flight, when a large group of returning soldiers walked past. As I stood to applaud them, everyone in the area joined in to welcome them home. The soldiers silently passed by, but it was obvious by their blushing and smiling faces that they truly appreciated it. They were happy to be home and rightly so.

Then thoughts of the Vietnam war and how shamefully and dispicably our returning soldiers had been treated by so many Americans came to mind. Is it any wonder that the veterans were loathe to discuss their experiences, when they were spat upon, and branded as monsters and baby killers by those who wouldn't serve to defend this country under any circumstances. Drafted to go to Vietnam, I was rejected for physical reasons. I can only try to imagine the horrors our soldiers had to endure. It was not a military campaign, but a politician's farce. Enlisted men and women and draftees alike performed extraordinarily under nightmarish condition, with one hand tied behind their backs by Washington. I know many vietnam veterans, who, when they would finally discuss the war, said that our military rarely lost a battle, but were never allowed to take the offensive that would have ensured victory.

Having been to the Vietnam Memorial in Washington several times, it has always been a somber experience witnessing the war veterans, and it is obvious who they are, reaching out to touch a name on that wall with tears in their eyes after all these years. They may cry for the loss of a comrade in arms, but they should never cry over or apologize for their brave efforts and the way they conducted themselves in Vietnam. This letter may bring back sad memories for veterans and their families, and I apologize for that, but this needs to be said. That war was not a black mark on the military's history, but rather a disgrace on the politicians and feckless Americans who treated our heroes with such disdain. Shame on them.

Don Maresca Sun City
My friend

REFLECTIONS OF
REDCATCHERS TODAY

On Jul 18, 2015
LARRY BRIDGMAN

Patti,

I want to take a moment and tell you a little about myself. I know you want to know about some of the men that spent the short time we had with George. Wayne Garrett and I are from the same home town. We both were drafted in May 1968. We left our home town of Duncan Oklahoma that May morning with about 100 other 19 year olds. We were sent to Fort Polk, La. There were 5 of us that knew each other out of that 100 plus. We all 5 were assigned to the same Basic Training company. Then when our orders came for AIT training, Wayne and I were assigned to the same company. The other 3 lucked out and got Clerk School, but we got infantry.

We received our orders for Viet Nam so we flew to Oakland California together. Then with 200 + we were by GOD's grace sent to Nam together where we all landed at Long Ben. After about 3 or 4 days they called out names for all the Unit replacements and then GOD stepped in again and put Wayne and me both in the 199th. A week at Redcatcher and we were assigned to our company. They put us both in Delta 4/12.

When we arrived at our Company there were (6) E1, (1) E5, (1) E6 and (2) 2nd Lt... We were put in the 2nd platoon. So Wayne and I were still together. That is when I met Fred Dyke. Patti he is the Fred from Tennessee that George spoke about.

The time of year was about the end of October or 1st of November. January 10th our company was sent to the bridge that George spoke about. The day we arrived they sent 2 squads from 2nd platoon out on patrol. That (1) E5 was my squad leader. We lost him that day from a booby trap. George arrived at the bridge somewhere close to the end of February. Then we moved our company down river and built our company base called Elvira. The day we got to our company in October, I was assigned the duty of carrying the platoon radio. Patti, when we moved to Elvira I had carried the radio for 4 months so I volunteered to carry a M60 machine gun. That's when George got my radio. He became platoon RTO. I took R & R somewhere around

March 14-20th as best as I can remember. That was a devastating week for Delta 4/12.

In your book, the last letter from George was dated March 16th. On March 17th our platoon sent out 2 squads on ambush. That night we lost 7 men. They set up on the rice patty dykes and the V.C. had them booby trapped. The next day is when we lost George. When I got back to my company headquarters from R & R, I was told about everything. I couldn't wait to get back to the company.

Patti, I'm not sure who Glenn was. We had so many new people coming in. I'm pretty sure Glenn is the guy we called Gomer! He resembled Gomer Pyle and would act like him for laughs. Gomer carried the mine detector for the company. Just before I went on R & R., Gomer found a large cache of enemy weapons and ammo. I feel sure this was Glenn, but I'm sorry to say I don't know any more about him. But I know the Fred from Tennessee that George spoke of, has to be Fred Dyke. I know Fred got shrapnel in his check and arm when Glenn or "Gomer" got hurt. Remember I was on R & R when this happened. Wayne, Fred and I were real close over there. I'm thankful that I have Wayne to see every day here at home. I could go on and on but I'll stop with this. I can't help you with Glenn, but I can give you Fred Dyke's address and phone. I'm sorry, but I don't have an E-mail for him. I've tried several times to find Fred over the years. I do know he was from Tennessee and last year I found him on the internet.

Patti, I talked to Fred one Sunday night on the phone. I know it has been 46 years, but some things you don't forget. Fred seemed like he didn't remember me. I've been pretty disturbed by it. He did send me a Christmas card after I sent him one. I hope he can help you. Maybe he will know Glenn's last name.

Patti, I hope that this has helped you in some way. If I can help you further please let me know.

GOD bless and I'll be looking for that new book, (I had to borrow Wayne's)

Larry

From: Patricia Enyedy <penyedy@yahoo.com>
Date: July 22, 2015
To: LARRY BRIDGMAN
Subject: Re: 199th, Delta 4/12

Larry

I was so pleased for you to share your story. Wayne has been a brother to me since my book was published.

How special to serve with your forever friend.

I think Gomer is probably Glenn. No one knows his last name or first name for that matter. I don't think George would have called him by his last name.

May I use your email in my book? I will use it in my section of Redcatchers reflections. I just made my reservations for next year's 50th reunion in Ft Benning. They are on their third hotel so they will have a good turnout. Do you think you and Wayne can attend? It is important a Gold Star Sister is there to represent the fallen. It is inspiring to me to know you all remember your fallen brothers. I love hearing you all lived wonderful lives.

I have lived with depression for many years so I know what it is like.

Losing my husband in 2014 and my mom 6 months later was very hard. So connecting with all of you and old friends again is very healing for me.

I hope we keep in touch.

Patti

Jul 27 at 6:34 PM
Patti,

Yes, I would be honored for you to use my story in your book.

I spoke with Wayne this morning about the reunion this next year, he would like to try and come. Donna and I would like to come and we will get together and visit more about it with Wayne and Nikki, but I know we need to make reservations as soon as possible. I will try also to get Fred Dyke to come. I plan to contact him and hopefully get him interested also.

Patti, I am so sorry for the loss of your Mother and husband. I will try to stay in touch with you from time to time. Looking forward to meeting you one day.

Your brother in Arms,
Larry

To Wayne

I got an email from Larry the other day. He told me how the two of you are childhood friends who went to Nam together. He thinks Glenn was a guy you called Gomer. Do you remember him? I can't tell you how happy you all make me by treating me like a Redcatcher sister. I just made reservations for the Redcatcher reunion next June at Ft Benning. I am working on my book.

Talk to you soon.
Patti

To
Patricia Enyedy
Jul 24 at 3:19 PM

Yes I do remember the guy we called Gomer! It had to be Glen. Larry and I talked about it. Me and Larry were childhood friends and still are the best of friends and finally got together after we both retired. Larry and I were drafted together went to Fort Polk thru Basic and AIT. Were sent to Vietnam together and they put us both in the same squad same company D-4-12 199th we were so glad they we were together. Larry and I go to the Chickasaw center and play a lot of pool. He will be my Brother always. I told Larry about you Patti and let him read the book I bought from you. He remembered things that I could not and I remembered things he could not. Me and Larry were always fighting side by side and watching each other's back.

Talk to you soon,

LARRY BRIDGMAN

Reflections of Bob Fromme, a Redcatcher with the LIB Delta 4/12. He was gracious enough to share these memories of his time in Vietnam with me. He did not know George but replaced him in the field the following month. In George's letters he describes his arrival at the base. Bob fills in the details in his articles he wrote years later.
Jul 24 2015

Patti,

As I mentioned over a decade ago in our first communication, I was drafted into the United States Army in 1969. After Basic Training and Advanced Infantry Training, at Fort Lewis, Washington, I was sent to South Vietnam to serve with the 199th Light Infantry Brigade. Over the course of the first weeks, my job was that of a Rifleman in a seven man squad in Delta Company, Fourth Battalion, and Twelfth Infantry. When our M60 Machine Gunner burned out and had to be moved to the rear, my job got a lot heavier as I was placed under that weapon. We spent the first months along the rivers, canals, and rice and pineapple fields between Saigon, "The Parrot's Beak" and the Delta. Eventually, we were moved into the mountainous area of abandoned rubber plantations and triple canopy jungle, between the village of Xuan Loc and the Sea. After nearly four months of war in the field, I was wounded by an enemy grenade and dusted-off to the field hospital at FSB Blackhorse. My recovery continued at the Brigade Main Base in Long Binh. Just before I was to be sent back out to the field, I decided to change my MOS and move to the Army Engineers where I would not have to carry a machine gun and where I hoped to use my college training and skill as and illustrator. I was sent to Chu Chi and then to Lai Khe, along the Cambodian Border, where I saw duty as a construction draftsman and jeep driver for

S3, Headquarters Company of the 554th Engineer Battalion, of the 20th Engineer Brigade.

Nearly thirty years later, I began to write about some of my memories from the war. After another decade, I was approached by "The Hoxie Sentinel", the local hometown newspaper in northwest Kansas concerning the possibility of sharing some of my memories from the War. The project grew into a series of weekly articles lasting nearly two years.

I will include an assortment from those articles and you can choose which ones you want to use, Patti. Some are long and may require being sent in sections.

Here is letter one.

Arrival Vietnam

Like most of the soldiers arriving in Vietnam, the air overwhelmed me as I walked out of the plane. The hot and humid atmosphere was the result of the equatorial proximity of the country. Next, came a strange assault of unpleasant smells floating in the thick air. Vietnam was about as "Third World" as one could imagine. Most of the country lacked the plumbing and infrastructure that we take for granted in the United States. One came to realize that everything in the country was in the process of rotting. The smell of human and animal excrement lingered all over. In addition, everyone was sweating and water for bathing was a luxury. In that air, one additional nuance to the stench resulted from the diet of the locals which full of strange and exotic foods and spices. So, as I walked out of the airplane and joined the other soldiers in formation on the tarmac the stench of the mold, the sweat, the excrement and the mysterious foods and spices floated in the mix of unbearable tropical heat. After several weeks, I got use to the smells. I don't think I ever adapted to the heat and humidity. To say the least, my life was becoming quite uncomfortable. A voice in my head said, "I don't think we're in Kansas anymore, Toto."

Within an hour, we were moved back into another plane. This time the craft had none of the luxury of the contract commercial transport that delivered us to the country. We were packed into a Fairchild AC-119 "Flying Boxcar". They had us so tight, when we were ordered to sit down on the floor, I wondered how I would ever get back up. Once seated, none of us could move. Soldiers had been pushed against each other, shoulder to shoulder and tummy to duffel bag.

With a belly full of men, the huge, roaring pollywog lumbered down the runway, struggling to find air. We had been issued a helmet but no weapon. I found myself pondering, "If we get hit while airborne and if I survive the crash, I won't have a weapon to defend myself". The thought soon faded and another problem presented itself.
Of all the places in the area within that plane, fate had placed me under a dip in the fluid lines that ran down the ceiling. The cool liquid caused a steady stream of condensation in the humid air. The drips chose their target at the top of my head. Drip, drip, drip, and drip again. I had removed the steel pot from my head but with the "water torture" thing going on, it went right back up there. The helmet tactic accomplished only one thing, the drips were now directed to the rear, into my collar and down my back. Pulled by gravity, the water was on a path of least resistance to the floor and my bottom. This shivering "Sad Sac" was soaked and seated in a puddle when we finally landed at Bien Hoa. When I remember that trip, cartoon images of "Beetle Bailey" come to mind.

The real comedy began as the aircraft landed and soldiers were ordered out. The cramped position had nearly everyone in a pickle. Our legs had gone to sleep. Men were struggling to stand, straggling and falling time and again, trying to move out. One man's legs would buckle. On his way to the floor, either he, or his duffel bag, would knock into his neighbor. And soon we were all falling like dominoes in the belly of the aircraft. I am sure this whole scene would not rank as one of our US Army's finest hours. Eventually we all made it to our feet and into the light of day

ELVIRA, FIRST IMPRESSION

The cattle truck pulled up to the gate of the little fire support base. I saw three large rolls of concertina snaked around the entire parameter of the base and across the road to form the gate. A guard dragged the long wire barrier back and over toward one side to let the truck enter the compound. The concertina gate bounced and jiggled in the dust like a stack of huge tethered "Slinkys". Once inside, the truck driver stopped and read my name from the orders on his clipboard. I climbed out the back of the truck and pulled my duffel bag out behind me. Several boxes of ammunition and C-rations were unloaded before the driver put the truck in reverse and backed toward the gate. The long wire barrier was pulled back open just in time for the truck to pass through. As the truck turned and headed on down the road, the wire gate was dragged closed and the camp parameter was again secure.

I stood for a few seconds surveying the place and waiting for someone to give me direction.

The little fire support base was organized in a triangle with a few bunkers along each of its three sides. In the center there were deep trenches with mortar tubes and shells stacked in the ready. One of the sides sloped with its bunkers facing a large canal. Part of the earth in and around the camp was barren from defoliation. Dust seemed to rise with every bit of movement. Along the tops of the bunkers were the silhouettes of guards on duty. Many of the men were shirtless. Most of them were wearing the floppy "jungle hats" instead of helmets. A few of the men were standing and looking out toward the horizon. Others were seated or recumbent. One of the soldiers on the roof of the nearest bunker appeared to be sun bathing. Some men were working along the parameter of concertina wire, fastening trip flares and checking the integrity of the camp's margin.

M-16 rifles were leaned together to form tee-pee shaped stacks outside the bunkers. Boxes of bandoleers and ammunition magazines were piled nearby. I could see several M-60 machine guns next to a nest of unboxed ammo belts for the guns. Down the line, several large bags of M-79 grenades had been placed in row. Four M-79 grenade launchers were lined up near the grenades. Along the line, were accumulations of pineapple grenades, baseball grenades, white phosphorous grenades, and assorted colors of smoke grenades? There was a pile of Claymore mines, firing devices, boxes of C-4 plastic explosive, blasting caps, and detonation cord for the explosives. Three small bazooka-like M-72 Light Anti-Tank Weapons were in the arsenal. Along the awkward order were groupings of "steel pots"(helmets), flak jackets, and field packs. Another stack of equipment appeared to be mine sweepers. Several PRC-25 field radios were also placed in order. One could also see wired cardboard boxes of C-Rations and several cases of soda and beer. I noticed that the same sort of accumulation could be seen out in front of the bunkers on the other two sides of the triangular camp.

I remember wondering to myself why all of this deadly stuff was kept out in the open instead of in the bunker. Later, I would realize that there was not enough room in the small bunkers. As a matter of logic, if "incoming" rockets and mortars began exploding in the small camp, you certainly did not want to be in the bunker along with all the explosives. In time, we also learned when we needed the tools of war, day or dark, we had a better chance of finding what we needed when they were roughly organized in open storage.

I continued to study the camp. A trailer tank had been unhitched and orphaned at the edge of the road near the mortar pits. On the side of the tank were stenciled the words, "potable water" in black paint. My visual examination widened. I could see a faded green wooden "six hole latrine" near the far end of the camp.

In the camp, there were clusters of men seated around empty ammo boxes, playing cards. Other men were talking and joking in small groups of six or seven. A few men were playing their adaptation of the game called **"Mumblety-peg".** One man would throw his bayonet to stick into the ground a few inches away from his opponent's feet. At each turn of the throw, the other opponent had to step out to the location of the dagger throw. Eventually, one of the men in the game would have his legs so wide that he could no longer keep his balance. He would fall backward or on his face. The group would laugh. The fallen man would get back on his feet and dust himself off. A new challenger would move into face the winner.

A short distance down the line, a pet monkey could be seen playing in the dust with a small brown and white spotted puppy. Both had collars and the monkey drug a leash.

Eventually, one of the soldiers came over to me. He could tell I was a little bewildered with the strange environment. The soldier said I should wait for Sergeant Ellias.

Staff Sergeant Eugene Ellias was a tall, thin, soft-spoken black man who had served as a drill sergeant in the States prior to his tour in Vietnam. He walked over, introduced himself and walked with me over to the camp headquarters. After a very quick introduction to Lt. Peter Joannides, the Platoon Leader, I was placed in the Second Squad of the Third Platoon. The Squad Leader, Corporal Routte walked me over to their portion of the platoon's bunker and introduced me to the other men in the squad. After my eyes adjusted to the darkened interior, I noticed that the men were laying on poncho liners. A few had been dozing when we walked in. One man had situated himself so that light from the entrance fell into his lap where he was reading a letter from home.

Cpl. Routte, told me where to put my duffel bag and suggested that I try to get some sleep. He said, "It is our night to do Bush and you're going to need a 16". He ducked out of the bunker. I understood that a 16 was probably an M-16 rifle. I had no idea what he was saying about a "bush". I had to ask one of the other soldiers what Routte meant by "Bush". I was informed that the squad would be spending the night in an ambush position four or five kilometers outside Fire Support Base Elvira. The men told me they would start to "saddle up around fourteen" and be "humping it west by fifteen hundred."

Translated, this meant we would begin to get our gear ready about two in the afternoon and by three o'clock we would be walking out of the camp and heading west toward the night's ambush site.

Corporal Routte returned. He mentioned that he had located a rifle for me. He seemed to sense that I was a bit concerned about the evening's work. He said, "Don't worry Fromme, just watch the rest of us and do what we do." Then he said, "Be sure and ask questions if you have a problem." As he stooped over and backed out the bunker entrance, he said, "Well look out for you until you get the hang of it, Newbie."

The men in the squad were correct. We started to pick up our gear and load weapons around two that afternoon. The men in the squad slowly picked themselves up walked out quietly to the piles of gear and weapons in front of the platoon bunkers. Each of them quickly had their gear together and ready.

I took a little longer. I had to connect the pack to the pack frame. I collected a poncho, poncho liner, towel, tooth brush, paste, soap, canteen, water, c-ration, insect repellent, bayonet, c-4 explosive, blasting caps, Claymore mine, firing device and wire. I was handed an M-16 rifle, two full magazines and a bandoleer of extra rounds. They also handed me a flak jacket, two pineapple grenades, one yellow smoke grenade and a belt of M-60 ammunition. When I asked about the ammo belt, they explained that riflemen had to carry at least one extra 60 belt since the gunner did not have and assistant to carry the extra ammo he needed. Watching the other men, I stuffed my floppy hat into my pack, put the blasting caps in my helmet band, and placed the C-4 in the longest leg pocket of my fatigues. According to one of the men, the point was to keep the caps as far away from the explosive as possible. I pulled on the flak jacket, shouldered the pack and put the helmet liner and helmet on my head. The grenades were attached to the front straps of the pack.

By three, we were headed out of the fire base. Corporal Ron Routte was in the lead, followed by his Radio Operator and the M-79 grenadier with his bag of bullets. One riflemen followed and then came the M-60 gunner. I walked behind the gunner and was followed by an experienced rifleman who would bring up the rear. The squad drew out when we were outside the gate. We walked single file with quite a bit of space between each man. . This was required infantry movement to avoid too many casualties at any one time if they opened up with automatic weapons' fire. The men walked quickly and very quietly. They communicated with hand signals and eye contact. When the squad stopped, each soldier stopped in place. Each man squatted, keeping the distance between him and the others.

DISCORD IN DELTA COMPANY

In spite of the importance of tolerance between soldiers at the bottom of the army, there seemed to be an air of continuing friction in Delta Company. I remember a sense of competition and some agitation between the four platoons. At times, there was discord between the squads within the platoon. An additional problem involved conflict between individuals. I do not know how much of the difficulty a natural result of stress from enemy activity around Elvira was. I do know that some of the men had issues that added to the stress around us.

A few of the men were in trouble with the law prior to service. In the 60's, it was a common practice for a judge in the U.S. to offer a second chance for a young man in trouble.... as long as, he joined the service. It was a tactic that usually got the young troublemaker out of town and into a more structured environment. Of course, if the fellows survived the training and were assigned to your unit in a combat zone, there was a good change that some of the "Leopards would not change their spots." Trouble had a way of following some of these men. At times you simply had to watch your back. A soldier like myself soon realized the value of being part of a squad where there were men you could trust. We learned to look out for each other, as well as, keep an eye on our collective stuff. C-rations, beer, water and weapons all seemed to grow legs if someone wasn't watching.

Soldiers in Delta Company had been gathered from all over the United States. The men came from varied economic and ethnic backgrounds. Among our population were activated National Guard soldiers of Asian heritage from Hawaii. We had soldiers with roots in Cuba and Puerto Rico. There were black men and white men from across the States. Some of the men were angry and self-serving. Some of the men seemed to thrive on the thrill of the hunt. They could also place you in danger. Some of the men saw the war as a chance to garner fame and rank within the military. They would get you killed. A few of the men in the unit had been dealt more than they could handle in the war. They had seen enough, suffered enough and were burned out. These individuals no longer cared about life. They were not the soldiers one wanted in the squad. They would sleep on guard duty and cover their incompetence under layers of lies. They made more work for everyone and they could get you or your buddies killed. Some of the soldiers carried the extra baggage of prejudice and hate. Occasionally some small thing would trigger a situation. Tempers would flare. The circumstance could quickly spin out of control.

One potentially deadly conflict between men in the platoon occurred in an afternoon after our squad had come in from "bush". The normal routine was to get the gear and weapons cleaned and stacked before taking "down time." Corporal Routte, our squad leader, had finished cleaning his M-16. He had it leaning up beside him as his attention turned to cleaning the rest of his gear. At that moment, another soldier named Jimmy came walking past. His foot caught the butt of Routte's freshly cleaned and oiled rifle. The weapon fell back into the dirt. Corporal Routte became enraged. Jimmy was a young tough black soldier from Gainesville Georgia, not the kind of fellow to walk away from confrontation. Like many of us draftees, he carried a sizeable chip on his shoulder. There is still some question in my mind concerning his actions with Routte's clean rifle. His kicking the butt of the weapon may not have been an accident but we will never know.

The upshot of it all was, the two men quickly got into a scuffle. The fist fight turned into a wrestling match. The men in the squad moved out of the way. Our unwritten policy was, as long as the men did not have weapons in hand, we would let them get it out of their systems. Fights served as a pressure release valve, of sorts. It was a way to ease some of the stress. Besides, afternoons in Elvira could become quite boring. A little entertainment and a chance to place bets on the winner was quite welcome.

Eventually, Lt. Joannides appeared. He barked out an order for the men to "break it up!" His order put both of the young soldiers off guard for a moment. The Officer positioned himself between the men. It was not long before Jimmy set his mind on getting around the Lt. in order to continue the fight. Corporal Routte was also ready to bring it all back on. The Lt. was quick to see the danger. Routte was ordered to "back off," which he did.

Lt. Joannides walked Jimmy down the incline toward the canal. He tried to reason with him. Then he realized that Jimmy had removed a pineapple grenade from his pocket. The young man was so worked up from the fight that he was not thinking straight. Jimmy looked down and realized that he had pulled the pin on the explosive. The confused and frightened soldier then threatened to "blow away" both Lt. Joannides and himself.

The Officer talked fast and furious with the young soldier. Eventually Joannides was able to get his hand over Jimmy's hand on the grenade. In due time, Castleberry agreed to let loose.

The situation seemed to be easing with the sign of some cooperation from Jimmy. Unfortunately, just as the grenade was exchanged into the hand of the Lt. the un-pinned handle came flipping up. The grenade was armed. The quick thinking Joannides heaved the thing up and out toward the canal below Elvira. I remember seeing the splash with the explosion. Soon there were a dozen dazed and dyeing fish floating on the canal after the blast. Fortunately they were the only victims of the escalating conflict of tempers on that particular afternoon.

Jimmy was allowed to stay in our unit. Eventually, after experiencing more of the war, the young soldier came to realize that his survival depended on others as much as we depended upon him. He, like the rest of us, matured, gained some control over our anger and accepted the duty we were handed.

TIME TO THINK

There was plenty of time to think in the quiet of the recovery tent that afternoon. Serenaded by the soft snoring of fellow with the concussion on the cot across the aisle, my thoughts ranged a wide and disturbing path. I began to worry about the folks at home. Like millions of families in the US, they were probably caught in their own personal struggles because of the war in Vietnam. I began to wonder what would happen if they were informed that I was in a hospital. Even though my wound was minor, without talking to me and without facts, their imaginations would race. I decided that I should write them a note so they would not worry over some "worst case scenario" conjured out of the cryptic government notification. Then I thought, perhaps they would not be informed at all....until I was dead. I rolled the questions over in my head for a while before settling on the side of a letter. My next step would be to try to talk one of the attendants out of some paper, a pencil, and an envelope. The attendant was not at hand. That project was put on hold.

Later, when the letter was written and sent, it would prove to be the only notification the family would receive. The Army sent them nothing. In irony, my family would fear the worst for the weeks following my letter, thinking that I would naturally try to play down the seriousness of any wound.

Back in the hospital tent, with time on my hands, more turbulence installed itself between my ears. The theme of the hour was fixed on trying to figure out how I had gotten into this predicament. I remembered the frustration and anger that came with the draft. The selfish and narrow voice in my head had me wondering why I had been chosen when so many of the local boys my age escaped conscription. As far as I could tell, those fellows were just as healthy. I revisited old issues considered at the time of the draft. Was it truly my bad "luck of the draw" or was something more sinister afoot? While in college, I had heard numerous accounts of "under the table" deals, expensive and bogus medical afflictions, and a menagerie of other ploys that were used by the unscrupulous to escape the draft. I had rejected the options of going to Canada or of taking a prison sentence in protest. All of that, Canada or prison, would have taken courage and commitment. I had neither. At that time, this was not my war. Our family had moved away from Sheridan County and the community that drafted me. In the paranoia of youth, the voice in my head wondered if perhaps it was easier for the people on the local draft board to send one who was no longer their own. That way, if things turned out bad, they did not have to risk facing the surviving family members on the street for years after they had done their work.

I lay on the cot considering my own scruples. After months in the field, learning how the war would profoundly alter a person, I wondered if I would have been so quick to capitulate honorably to the call of a nation and that of the local daft board. I recalled that military service was forced on me. When I agreed to give up two years of my life it was not an issue of being driven by any particular patriotic zeal. At the time, I certainly was not looking for any 'big adventure'. Back in 1968, I simply wanted to get on with graduate school. Later, when the draft notice came in the mail I realized that my family, especially my father, would catch volumes of unfavorable attention if I ran from the orders. Two years before, the Governor had appointed Dad to fill a position on the Kansas Supreme Court. My parents were honorable, Christian people and they certainly did not deserve the agony of negative criticism from the vultures of the Press in Topeka and around the State. Such would have been the case had a son of a state judge not taken what was considered to be the honorable response to the draft.

Staring up at the billowing olive drab tent fabric above my hospital cot, I came to one harsh reality. When confronted by the draft, in ignorance and without real conviction about the war, I had quietly accepted my fate and it had taken me to the unfortunate present. With the draft, others, uncaring strangers, were taking possession of my life and I was too young and too foolish to realize what was really happening. At the time that decision was made, I had no idea where

I was actually headed. At best, accepting the draft was probably an effort on my part to try to do the right thing in a "no win" situation. At worse, I had been really, really stupid to let myself get shoved into the middle of this absurdity called war. Why had I been so quick to risk assignment to the infantry just to get out of the military in two years? I decided only an extraordinarily stupid person should ever have to ask themselves a question like that?

In the months following the draft, there had been plenty of time to learn the life of an infantryman. That life was dragging humanity out of me, turning me into some kind of animal operating on basil survival instinct. I was sick of it. The irrational behavior when I realized they had taken my weapon at the operating table was a symptom of larger psychological changes within. Where in all of this was the quiet young college student looking forward to a future in the Visual Arts? What had happened to that fellow? Where was he in all of this? Perhaps he was right there with me in the hospital tent, fighting for his own psychological survival.

I knew after the hospital, if I returned to the field they would have me right back out in the jungle under the M-60, running with the medic into the next fire fight.... and then the next. A time would come when my luck would be used up. I was sick of it, all of it. My emotion were amplified knowing our own leaders in Washington had no intention of trying to win the struggle they had us in. The news of Nixon's plan for troop reduction and his failure at the Paris Peace Talks amplified my frustration. It was all such a waste.

There were the blundering mistakes of the officers and other soldiers to consider. Memory took me back to the confusion of coordinates that yielded the artillery rounds dropping onto our location. Then there was the Cobra pilot and his mini-gun. Grief lingered from the so-called "friendly fire" at Hoc Mon when James Reasons and Melvin Johnson were killed. On top of that abhorrence were the tragic and avoidable deaths of Dave Kenney and Claude VanAndel when their squad had been ordered into the ambush just two weeks prior. I thought about SSG Andujar, wondering how long it would take for the government to notify his family. There were all the men who had been wounded. That list was growing much longer. I remembered Stanley Markusen at Hoc Mon, Ron Cone, the Dog handler, the "Kit Carson Scout", the black Sergeant and the others near Ben Luc. The "Casualty Read Out" in my head continued with the names of buddies; Barret, Doc Reppart, Nixon, Cope, Weaver, Rufino, Gilreath, and Charles Fink from the May 27th ambush and now they would add my own name to that list. Soon it would be too difficult to remember all of us. Even worse, some of us may end our service in Delta Company with the dubious distinction of being on both lists.

I contemplated the names and remembered a few good times with the buddies. One wondered if our paths would cross once more.

I thought about Ron Routte, Mike Scott and Carl Belmont, the three remaining men from our squad in the field. It was bad enough when we were down to four out of the original seven. Now, with only three of them, they had to be under unbearable stress. Their plight was very disturbing, but there was not much that I could do to help them out. A prayer did not seem like much to offer, but it was all I had at the time. From my hospital cot, I quietly handed their struggle to the Lord.

There were many questions to consider. Did my future have to be called 11 Bravo (Light weapons Infantryman)? Could I take advantage of my time out of the field to find something better for myself? What would I need to do to secure a less-violent future? Then and there, in the field hospital at FSB Blackhorse, part of the ignorance of my youth slid behind me. I decided it was time to take some responsibility for generating more reasonable direction in my life.

The second afternoon passed, syncopated by the trembling fabric of the hospital tent shaking from an occasional breeze and the wind of choppers. Med-Evacs, terror taxies, came and went. The cots of our recovery tent filled. Wounded soldiers came and went. Some with injuries more insignificant then my own. Others, more critical, were held in the ward until they could be moved to a larger hospital in Saigon, in Japan or back in the States. Late afternoon turned to evening and then into night. Days spent on the cots, playing cards, became boring and long. There was too much time to think and too few options to think about.

On the evening of the third day I noticed a familiar face as one young soldier came limping down the aisle between the cots. It was the same fellow from Delta Company that I had seen in the field, days before the firefight, trying to infect the blister on his heel with a hand full of dirt. He must have succeeded in his project. He was out of the jungle.

I could see that every step was excruciating for him. He fought back tears and seemed to be paying with pain for every inch of his slow progress down the aisle toward his cot. I started to speak up and then caught myself. I wanted nothing to do with the kid. I had nothing but contempt for him and others like him. Individuals like this were as much the enemy of survival as was "Charlie". Out in the field they placed their own selfish agenda ahead of their buddies. Perhaps I should have pitied the man, but disdain was the only emotion that I could muster. He was reaping his own just reward in that manufactured suffering. No doubt his tour in country would be an endless string of schemes and scams devoted to shirking his duty and destroying any remaining thread of his own self-respect. Unfortunately, he would probably survive the year, catch the freedom bird and concoct his war stories with the same fertile imagination that had him in his current world of pain. This, while better men like VanAndel, Kenney and Andujar would die for duty, for honor. In country, every man seemed to be fighting their own personal war and the nature of the war they fought was often a reflection of their own character. I wondered if every war was like this one.

There was little to do at the hospital. On the morning of the fifth day Scott's M-16 joined the other pile of dirty belongings below my cot. One would think that they could at least wash my cloths. I was told that was not their job, however, the orderly did say they would keep me until the afternoon and then I could return to my unit.

The morning was filled with anticipation. This soldier was ready for a change. I busied myself with the molding pile of filth under my bunk.

Anything washable in my ruck, as well as my torn shirt, jungle boots and fatigue pants were taken out to the shower. I found a partial bar of soap in the mud between the pallet planks at the floor of the booth and while still wearing the hospital garb, I furiously set about scrubbing everything. The wash dried quickly spread out over several empty fifty-gallon drums near the tent. By noon, I was sitting back at the cot, dressed for the field, ready to go.

There I sat. Nothing happened. At two in the afternoon I caught an orderly to remind him that I was to be released. He told me they knew that and I should just be patient. I waited.

Around three thirty the orderly came in to change the bandages and give me instructions for medicating and bandaging the wound on my own. I decided I would probably need help with the process he described with my wound being located back at my shoulder blade. He also informed me that they were trying to line up a ride to get me back to my unit. I waited again.

Early in the afternoon the fellows in the tent seemed sympathetic to my long delay, as the old Army cliché, "hurry up and wait" ordered my day. The attitude of consolation turned to amusement as the hours wore on. One of the fellows down the aisle blurted out, "What's the rush, Grunt.....You got a 'boom-boom girl' waiting back in Saigon?"

The tent was filled with laughter. His comment initiated a string of similar amusing jabs as another soldier on a cot near the door of the tent shouted back, "Naah, old Grunt heard his wife was stepping out on him while he won this here week at the Red Cross Hotel.... his kids are calling some stranger, Daddy." He's got to get home to set them straight!"

The fellow on the cot across the aisle from me came back with." You (expletives omitted) have it all wrong, can't you see Charlie blew his head off. He got a million dollar hit and he is on his way back to the States. You would be in a hurry too if you were headed for the 'Freedom Bird'."

There was a pause as we all contemplated the thought of going back home.

The silly tales conjured in the minds of bored patients picked up once again. If the soldiers on the hospital cots were not asleep or unconscious, ache of them seemed to have some new and unique concoction of an imaginary reason why I was in such a hurry to get out of the hospital. The crazy stories continued. Some were very inappropriate and will not be repeated.

In spite of the fact that it was being directed at me, like the others in the tent, I found their banter amusing. Hospital life had become a drag and here, in the last few seconds, these fellows had me in Saigon with a prostitute; married with children; on my way back to the States on the 'Freedom Bird' with my head blown off, and possibly made a eunuch by a VC bullet. When the stories and the laughter died down I shook my head. For lack of anything imaginative to offer, I simply said, "you fellows are something else." To which came the prompt reply from the man next to me, "Fromme, you sorry (expletive omitted), we all know you love living in the boonies so much you can't wait to go home to the jungle. In turn, I replied, "Truth would have it, I can't wait to get out of here and away from all you raggedy-(expletive omitted) losers."

We all laughed again.

When the chaff in the tent settled down, I stretched out on my stomach on the cot, closed my eyes, and took a nap. An hour before dusk I was awakened by a man sticking his head in the tent and yelling, "We have a ride for the 199th....Redcatcher, you ready?" I said goodbye to the fellows while I put on my boots, scooped up the ruck, the steel pot, the flak jacket and the M-16. Out the door of the tent I went. The last those fellows saw of me was the old rip up my shirt flapping in the breeze over the wide bands of white tape and bandages on the grenade wound in my back.

GOING NOWHERE FAST

The jeep was parked to the side of the base camp road near the hospital with the motor running. The driver and another soldier were seated in front, so I had to climb over several boxes to take a place in the back. There was no time to negotiate with the packages for a comfortable position before we were off with a jerk, through a labyrinth of dusty roads and trails. We worked our way around assorted compounds and down the hill toward the southern edge of the base.

Several weeks earlier, my platoon had been transported into this part of the camp by truck. We had the luxury of sleeping in the screened hooch's over night before moving out again to the jungle. The area was constructed on the side of a hill. The cluster of hooch's were far enough below the road so that only the tin roofs were in view. The driver missed the stop, hit the brakes, slid to a standstill and slammed his stick in reverse. We backed out of our own billowing dust cloud moving faster than any sane person would try to drive in reverse. We raced back around the hill in reverse until we came back up to a spot on the road above the cluster of tin roofs. Again, he hit the brakes and we slid to a stop. I rolled out over the boxes with the M-16, and the rest of my gear. As soon as my feet were on the road, before I could tell the fellow thanks for the lift, the spinning back tires of the jeep were tearing at the road, enveloping me in a cloud of dust and pelting me with gravel.

Casting a long shadow from the evening light, I stood alone. The setting sun had carved out a beautiful lattice of orange and red tracts of sky between silver clouds along the horizon. I walked over to the path which wound its way down the hillside to the hooch's. This part of the fire support base seemed unusually quiet. I worked my way down the path and my sense of the quiet seemed stronger. The compound appeared to be empty. One by one, the wobbling old screen doors were opened and then closed. I moved down through the cluster of hovels, conglomerations of sandbags, lumber, screen and tin. All were empty. There was no sign that the area had been inhabited for days. Feelings of extreme loneliness settled over every inch of my being.

As I contemplated how to deal with my little crisis, a haggard, ashen rat crept out of the shadows and worked his way up the stack of sandbags to take a perch on the top layer of the barricade around the hooch beside me. It paused. Slowly it raised itself on hind quarters, sniffed at the air, and contemptuously appraised this lonesome and confused stranger trespassing its territory. It was a sorry excuse for a rodent. One of its ears was torn into strips which hung out flopping along at the side of its head as he moved. It had a scar across its nose and several old wounds or soars on one of its front legs. The thing was tormented by fleas. It scratched at its stomach and took to a fit of shaking its head vigorously as if they were deep in its ears. As it lowered itself and turned to sneak on down to the back of the barricade, I noticed the thing was missing part of the pad and claws on one of its swollen hind feet.

The pathetic creature started me thinking of the beaten cadaver of an NVA soldier I had seen one Sunday morning laying at a crossroads in the delta village of My Yen. The poor fellow seemed to have been through a living hell. His shirt and shorts were in tatters. He looked as if he had lost, or warn off, his sandals. His emaciated legs ended with bandaged feet and ankles covered with open cuts and bruises. The little soldier looked as if he had starved to death on his way down from his home in the North. The memory was repugnant. The image of the corps lingered and frequently haunted me to the point of pitying this enemy soldier. I had to keep reminding me that the man and his kind would have taken my life, or that of a buddy, in a heartbeat. He was the enemy. He was not deserving of my pity.

Standing alone in the darkening cluster of sandbag lined shacks I refused to contemplate that soldiers suffering, his dedication to his own country or his demise. I had to face my own problem. For a while, I toyed with the idea of staying the night on the floor of one of the hooch's. Perhaps someone from my unit would be there to pick me up in the morning. The thought was quickly dropped when I considered that there was no indication that the place had been occupied for days. Obviously the unit had moved. No doubt a mistake had been made when they discharged me from the hospital. My cogitation evaporated with the thought of setting up in the same camp with that old ragged hungry, possibly rabid rat. It was probably already drooling at the thought of feasting on my ears, fingers, toes, or any edible thing that might slip out from under the poncho liner wrapping of my sleep. It was settled.... I would not stay there. I would retreat from that bit of country and leave it to that old battle scared native, that old Vietnamese veteran of many base camp garbage can battles. As far as I was concerned the old scruffy rodent had probably earned his territory. He could have it. He could have the whole country as far as I was concerned.

I came back up the hillside trail and onto the road above. By the time I was up the incline, the world was fully dark. Then, I noticed several stars had come out to meet the distant evening noises of the base camp. The first illumination rounds of the evening tore into the calm and whizzed out over the concertina wires of the camp perimeter. The rounds exploded high above and began to light my way along the secluded road. I walked up to the high ground in search of the closest lighted tents or hooch's. When these were located, I continued in their direction. Soon the humidity of my eventide hike had beads of sweat rolling out from under my helmet. Large dark patches of wet had grown on my shirt by the time I walked into the C.Q. hooch of the nearest unit. Their big nightly command-quarters poker game was paused as I told them my story. I tried to sound official as I explained that I was part of the Third Platoon, Delta Company, 4th Battalion 12th Infantry, and 199th Light Infantry Brigade. I asked for some advice on how to locate my unit and where I could sleep the night.

Their First Sergeant broke out laughing so hard that he spilled some of the whiskey from the Dixie cup he was holding. I could barely understand the old man as he groaned out his pleasure at my predicament. He turned to the Staff Sergeant next to him and said," Hell, I've heard of losing a soldier or two, even a squad, but this 'Swinging (expletive omitted)' has lost a whole grunt brigade.

The laughter in the little shack eventually ceased. The card game continued. I was invited to spend the night on an extra cot in the C.Q. shack and they promised to help me deal with my problem in the morning. As the game moved along the participants worked on the magnitude of their inebriation. In turn, like a stray dog in their hut, in their night, I crawled onto their extra cot and fell asleep.

At dawn, snooze ended in the quandary of unfamiliar surroundings populated by strangers. I was not the only confused soldier in that place. My situation was complicated by the realization that the faded, aqua vitae memory of their First Sergeant held no recollection of my arrival the previous evening. He wanted to know why I was there, sleeping in his Unit. In fact, his hangover and short temper made it difficult for me to restate my predicament and to communicate my need to find a way back to Delta Company or, at least, some unit of the 199th. Fortunately one of the staff sergeants in the card game had been sober enough in the previous evening to remember my arrival. He was successful in his attempt to remind his superior of their offer of a cot and the promise to help get me back to my unit.

By mid-morning, the company clerk was on the radio searching for a transportation company with a truck headed for the 199th Brigade Main Base at Long Binh. Soon, I was part of the truck cargo that went bouncing out the gates of FSB Blackhorse and off toward brigade headquarters.

The trip was only about forty kilometers, however, pedestrians, ox carts, bicycles and bad road translated into several hours in the back of the truck. The journey would have been uneventful had it not been for two ARVN (Army of the Republic of Vietnam) soldiers. The little fellows timed the passing of our truck with a barrage of M-16 fire as we started over a bridge. In a heartbeat, instinct had me in a dive for cover. I went sliding and then prostrate below tumbling boxes in the bed of the truck. As we moved on past, I could see them through the lower slats of the truck's tailgate. There was really no danger. The two Vietnamese soldiers were amusing themselves with a bit of target practice at fish in a river below. I felt a bit foolish working my way back up to a sitting position on a low stack of wobbling cargo. While the driver did his best to hit every bump and pothole in the long road between the bridge and the gates of Long Binh, I did my best to extract several splinters from the palm of one hand, remnants from my frightened dive onto the weathered bed.

At Long Binh It was the usual ritual of "standing-down". The M-16 had to be cleaned, inspected and checked it in with the NCO at the armory room. In the interchange, I was assigned a bunk. I also inquired about a baseball cap. No sir! I had not forgotten about the hat exchange rule of the base, thanks to the previous encounter with "Major Starched-shorts". I also asked the sergeant when he thought I would be headed back out to the field. He said when the hospital sends them back to BMB, we usually keep them a week for a little more R and R (Rest and Relaxation) before they go back out to the line company. With this bit of information, I realized time would be critical if I was going to take advantage of the situation and construct a change in the course of my life.

The following day was spent working through the possibilities. It seemed there were no "Rear Echelon" jobs available at the 199th. I checked out openings for base parameter guard, truck driver and company clerk. These were all filled and when they came available they usually went to men who had prior experience and training or to "short timers" with only a few remaining weeks before they were to be shipped back home.

My next option was to locate a reenlistment NCO assigned to the base. I had been thinking about trying to get into a field that would have some relationship to my college degree. At the very least, I wanted to try to get out from under the M-60. When I inquired about changing my MOS (Military Occupation Specialties) to something like combat artist, the sergeant was very frank about my chances. He explained I would need to sign up for four additional years. He added that the Army could only guarantee some kind of job in the broader field of graphics. I asked what jobs were included in that group. Among the jobs on the list he mentioned were construction draftsman, illustrator, topographer, cartographer, and model maker. To be honest, I was not sure about half of the things that he referred to in that field. The sergeant assured me that I would receive OJT (On the job training). He felt that with a college degree in a related field, I would probably be able to do any of the work in the range of graphics after a little training.

The information was encouraging. The thought of spending four more years in the Army was not as repugnant as it had been at the time of my draft. I knew I could handle the boredom and the regimen. In exchange for a little less violence in my life, I certainly knew that I could stomach a few more years of taking insults and orders.

Deteriorating developments out in the field were fresh in my memory. The jungle was inhospitable and dangerous place for all of us. The company was seriously under strength. Beneath the "pig", my existence had degenerated into the life of a pack mule or a slave and it was all for no reason. Nixon and the rest of the government had no sense of commitment, why should I? I had gambled with the draft and it was not working out. I had been ignorant and foolish. It all seemed to boil down to a matter of giving them four years of my life in exchange for a possible fifty additional years. Even if I could manage physical survival for the rest of the year, my grief over the men we had lost was not diminishing. Many times I tried and failed to block their images out of my mind. I decided that I could not take much more of it. It was becoming an issue of my own mental health.

In this young male mind, I considered the possibility of being labeled a coward if I reenlist in order to get out of the Infantry. After a little consideration, I felt like that was not much of an issue. After all we had been through, this soldier could certainly handle a little name-calling. I had done my job in the field as best I could, in spite of the danger. If I had any sense of guilt with the decision, it came with the realization that the three remaining men in the squad would have a more difficult time trying to make things work. Within the squad, each of us had talked about trying to get out of the field. I felt any one of my buddies would probably do the same thing, given the chance. I decided they would probably not hold it against me if I found a way out.

The following day I returned to the reenlistment NCO and told him I was ready to sign the papers for a job in Army graphics. By the end of the week, I knew I would be transferred to an Engineer unit for OJT as a Construction Draftsman. I was told that I would be assigned to some unit within of the 20th Engineer Brigade.

Thank you Bob for giving us an understanding of the soldier in the Vietnam War. I will be eternally grateful. Hope to see you at the reunion next year.

REFLECTIONS OF TODAY

I wrote to my nephew asking him to write a piece for my book, he just retired from the Army and was deployed 8 times since 9/11. He spoke Arabic, Farsi, he was in Civil Affairs.

That's fantastic, Aunt Patti. I hope you're closing in on finally getting Glenn's identity. One thing that occurs to me about being a vet today is how much we owe to the Vietnam vets. I don't believe most returning vets had shit thrown at them, or were actually called "baby killers" to their faces. At least that would have given them a focus for their anger and resentment. The reality was worse—they were simply ignored. All the pain and sacrifice, delayed and disrupted lives, and the dead buddies (and enemies), were merely shrugged off by the American people for whom they were supposedly fighting.

There can be nothing worse than being considered irrelevant. The belated recognition of that wrong, and America's well-deserved guilt over it, has ensured that the reception of recent vets is worlds different. Today, we have a professional, volunteer Army where soldiers return back to an infrastructure that gives us a continuing sense of mission and purpose, peers who have undergone similar experiences, and counseling for those in need; we're not given a bus ticket and thrown back into the pond cold. The Guard and Reserve must have it a little tougher in that respect.

Americans go out of their way, sometimes embarrassingly so, to come up to soldiers in uniform and thank them for their service. Once I got away from Fayetteville, where everyone's a vet of one kind or another, walking down the sidewalk in uniform made me feel like some kind of celebrity. It is much easier to reintegrate back into the real world now because the lessons learned from the Vietnam Era have been translated into better services, and a more gradual reintegration for today's returning veterans. Vietnam vets took a bullet for the rest of us. We, too, owe them our thanks.

LTC Jack McLaughlin, RET US Army

August 2015

Pat, I am sorry but this email will probably make you cry again.
First of all I am very sorry. I have been so absorbed in my own stuff
and these trips unfortunately,that I neglected to stay in touch with
you after your Mom passed away. I am truly sorry and sorry I could
not be there for you. But that is not the reason this email might bring
tears to your eyes.

I started to read your book on my last flight from Seoul to Shanghai
just a couple of hours ago. That book is so powerful. I had to stop
numerous times to wipe the tears from my eyes. From the first page
with George's picture in uniform I could not put the book down. I
got through about 80 pages before the flight landed and I had to
stop. The flight was 2 hours but I was mesmerized. Will finish the
last few pages tonight.

Of course being from Linden the connections were numerous but
frankly you are one heck of a writer. Powerful stuff, maybe because
you let your raw feelings come out -- all of them.

I don't know why I did not learn of your brothers passing for years,
maybe not even until you mentioned it when we first spoke some
months ago.

So many connections. You know my father was in WWII as your
Dad was and was stationed in Joplin, Missouri. He and my Mom got
married a few years before the war ended and as my grandparents
were from Linden, they moved back to this area. Had a little 2
bedroom unit in Elizabeth like your parents did and where I lived until
I was two when we bought the house on Summit Terrace. Maybe
we were neighbors.

There are a lot of other connections that I will speak with you about
sometime and you bringing George's life through his 20 years just
brought my upbringing in Linden so clearly back in focus.

One thing that stood out was the pain you and your family suffered. Unbearable. It hurts me to think of how you suffered and your Mom and Dad who never got past it but I guess nobody does. At least you found Elliott and had another Elliott as well and your daughter.

Patricia, George would have been so proud of you and that book. Sorry if you are crying but I am too.

Speak with you when I get back. Hope the funeral goes as easy as possible for you.

Love you,
Steve

PS, Gags was one heck of a friend, we should all have a friend that loyal. you and George both were/are lucky to have him.

Regarding Vietnam, yes, my company has a factory there that I have visited a couple of times, tomorrow as well. It is located outside of Saigon (now Ho Chi Minh city) but I do not know what direction. The river George referred to was probably the infamous Mekong Delta and our factory is near there. Last time I was here I was taken out by a young man and woman from the plant. He was from North Vietnam and she from the south, now boyfriend and girlfriend. If I get near that river on this trip I will try to take some pictures for you with my phone but not likely as I will only be there one day.

September 30, 2015

Steve Shur is my dear friend from Linden High School. I am so glad we found each other again after all these years. While he was in Saigon he bought me a beautiful book of pictures of Viet Nam. I love it so much.

This is a reflection of my brother Steve.

Since the death of my brother back in March of 1969 in Vietnam, it has been very difficult for me. I was a senior in Linden High School. I was proud to hear others talk so highly of him, but that's all I ever had. I miss him dearly for when I ever wanted to ask him a question, he wasn't there for me. It has been a very lonely life without him. He could have had a family and we could have celebrated the holidays together or even shared a beer on a hot sunny day.

He sacrificed his life for the freedom of us people in the USA. At age 64 now, I will see him again when THE LORD calls for me and then we will have that beer together. God Bless U Brother

Sincerely,

Stephen Farawell
September 25, 2105

October 1, 2015

First let me say that I'm honored that Patti asked me to write some words about George for her new book. I would like to start off by saying everyone should know how devastating it is to a family losing a loved one in a war. It is truly an indescribable hurt that lasts a lifetime. So, if in the future, you see an American soldier killed in the line of duty understand the long term effects that result from it.

I think of George often. This year I had a bout with throat cancer. I found myself praying and talking to George when I went for my diagnosis, radiation treatments and watching over me when they finished. I am happy to report I am cancer free. George never lets me down!

I often think about what a great husband and father George would have been. All these years later, anyone I run into from our Linden past always says what a great guy he was. There isn't a week that goes by that I don't think about how our friendship would have grown. I regret that my wife, Jennifer, and my daughter, Natalie, never got to now George. He would have been my daughter's Godfather for sure! You can be certain that a piece of my life was taken that day.

George Farawell was a great guy and my best friend. Just seeing how much love Patti has shown over the years for George is another example of the effect his death had on her. For me, I will think of him and keep praying to him as long as I live. To Patti, I hope and pray this book brings some peace to her. I am and always will be proud that her and her family loved me with all their hearts. Know that the feeling is mutual.

With Love,

Rich Gagliardi

MY REFLECTIONS

I am happy to say on September 25, 2015, there are additions to make.

My book brought Barbara and Ronnie together in 2001, they have married and have a wonderful combined family. They live in Florida.

My brother Steve remarried. I met Linda the day of my speech at the NJVM.

My grandkids have grown to be wonderful young adults. Tyler is 20 he is working and going to college. Courtney is 17 and a senior in high school. She is going to college next year.

Their pictures are included at the end of my book.

I am getting ready to go to my 50th Class Reunion in October. Where did the time go?

I have connected with old friends through writing this book. Facebook is a wonderful connecting tool.

This was a labor of love and I have connected with Redcatchers again, family and friends.

I look forward to going to the 50th Reunion of the Redcatchers next year as a Gold Star Sister in Ft. Benning GA where the Redcatchers Light Infantry Brigade originated.

I hope this book is a history lesson for our kids and grandkids about the war of our generation.

I hope I made George proud.

I would like to close with why this book means so much to me. My thoughts came flooding to me on Father's Day in June 2015. Missing my husband Elliott, who passed away in March 2014 my dad, and George. What kind of man and father would he have been. I know he would have been exceptional. He loved my parents, brother, his friends, family and me. He took time with each of us the last day before we took him to the airport. We had a quiet day just us with all the tears and pain. He lived through his family and friends who never forgot him.

As Richard said in his essay George would have been Natalie's Godfather, he also would have been my son Elliott's Godfather as soon as he got home. That letter came back to me.

We knew he would make us proud and he did. The words of love and friendship that reached out to us for years was astounding. People still contact me today about the book for their grandchildren.

I saved all these touching messages from day one. The boy from Linden NJ was never forgotten. He touched people in so many ways as you have read. Never forgotten by his comrades, The Redcatchers are an inspiration to all those brave men killed and wounded in their unit. They have respected and loved us all these years. I am so proud to be called a Gold Star Sister.

I have a recurring dream that I open the front door and see a bus in front of the house. There is George and his duffle bag as handsome as ever at 20 years old getting off the bus. I say to him ""where have you been?" He just smiles with that grin of his and takes me in his arms.

Amen.

One more thing at Thanksgiving dinner when my grandson just learned about my book. He was thankful for being on Gram's book cover. Tyler is now twenty working hard and going to school. I never forgot those words. Thank you Tyler.

Till I see you all again, mom is now with her boys, she is finally at peace.

October 2, 2015

Patti Farawell Enyedy August 7, 2015

Elliott, me and Amanda

**Bill and Amanda LaGrutta, Elliott and Mary
Beth Enyedy, Elliott and Patti Enyedy**

**Yolanda Carrion Bustamante and me at
Vietnam Memorial Wall in DC**

Courtney, Elliott, Mary Beth and Tyler Enyedy

Linda and Steve Farawell

**Amanda LaGrutta, my mom Mary
Farawell, me, and my son, Elliott.**

**My mom at her 100th birthday at Shallotte Assisted
Living in Shallotte, NC on October 7, 2014. She
passed away on December 18, 2014. She is now
with her boys. Miss you mom everyday.**

Vietnam Memorial Wall DC at Christmas

A special thank you to everyone who made this book possible, family, friends, Redcatchers and all Vietnam veterans over the past 45 years. Your thoughts and prayers have meant so much to the Farawell and Enyedy families.

October 27, 2015

PICTURES ON THE BACK COVER:

Left: Elliott Enyedy Jr. my husband, Marybeth Enyedy, my daughter-in-law holding Courtney Enyedy my granddaughter, Elliott Enyedy III my son, me, Tyler Enyedy my grandson, Mary Farawell my mother, Stephen Farawell my brother, Amanda La Grutta my daughter and Billy La Grutta my son-in-law in December 1999.

ABOUT THE AUTHOR

Patricia now lives in Hampton, NH with her daughter Amanda and Bill LaGrutta. You can contact her at penyedy@yahoo.com or on Facebook.

Printed in Great Britain
by Amazon

78157218R00144